Cooperative Co-Parenting
for Secure Kids

The
Attachment
Theory Guide to
Raising Kids in
Two Homes

Aurisha Smolarski, LMFT

New Harbinger Publications, Inc.

Publisher's Note

This publication is designed to provide accurate and authoritative information in regard to the subject matter covered. It is sold with the understanding that the publisher is not engaged in rendering psychological, financial, legal, or other professional services. If expert assistance or counseling is needed, the services of a competent professional should be sought.

NEW HARBINGER PUBLICATIONS is a registered trademark of New Harbinger Publications, Inc.

New Harbinger Publications is an employee-owned company.

Cover design by Sara Christian

Acquired by Jennye Garibaldi

Edited by Brady Kahn

Library of Congress Cataloging-in-Publication Data on file

Printed in the United States of America

26   25   24

10   9   8   7   6   5   4   3   2   1   First Printing

"Divorce and separation are a shock. Aurisha's practical exercises guide co-parents through the messy transitions and turbulent emotions to ease everyone through their upset and grief. Experiential activities offer self-awareness and opportunities to repair attachment wounds. When adults gain insight and skillfulness to heal themselves, children's secure attachment needs become prioritized with less stress—*despite deep divides and different attachment styles.* This brilliant book is a godsend in navigating divorce."

> —**Maggie Kline**, coauthor of *Brain-Changing Strategies to Trauma-Proof Our Schools, Trauma Through a Child's Eyes,* and *Trauma-Proofing Your Kids*

"As a licensed marriage and family therapist and divorced mom, Aurisha Smolarski knows how the bickering and battles of divorced parents can hurt a child. If you've been searching for the best guidance and tools for co-parenting, you've found the right book. Aurisha introduces the principles of secure attachment so you can form a cooperative team and improve your co-parenting approach for your child's benefit. This book is co-parenting gold."

> —**Stan Tatkin, PsyD, MFT**, developer of the Psychobiological Approach to Couples Therapy, and author of *Wired for Love* and *In Each Other's Care*

"*Cooperative Co-Parenting for Secure Kids* offers the guidance and insight co-parents need to provide security for their children, even in the midst of a separation. Smolarski's helpful exercises, grounded advice, and easy-to-grasp framework provide a road map to navigating interactions with each other and their child. I look forward to sharing this book with many families."

> —**Tina Payne Bryson, LCSW, PhD**, *New York Times* bestselling coauthor of *The Whole-Brain Child* and *No-Drama Discipline,* and author of *The Bottom Line for Baby*

"This book is so needed! One of the biggest stressors for parents after they decide to end their romantic relationship is how to continue parenting their kid(s). This is where Aurisha Smolarski's book comes in. She takes the fear and the stigma out of this challenging time and lays out a science-based, practical, and thoughtful guide to help parents offer a secure base for their child going forward."

> —**Kara Hoppe, MFT**, author of *Baby Bomb*

"Co-parenting is not easy, even if both partners are committed to putting their children's sense of security first. It's even harder when one or both parents is overwhelmed with anger, loss, or worry. This book provides a useful road map, based on a deep understanding of attachment theory. The core principles and practical strategies can help any co-parent get started on a healthy path, or course-correct to a better co-parenting relationship."

—**Lawrence J. Cohen, PhD**, author of *Playful Parenting* and *The Opposite of Worry*

"With thirty years in family law, I value awareness. Aurisha Smolarski's *Cooperative Co-Parenting for Secure Kids* is transformative. Highlighting co-parenting challenges and offering attachment theory-based solutions, it's more than a guide—it's a lifeline. Essential for families seeking a harmonious, restructured future."

—**Susan Guthrie**, leading family law attorney, mediator, and host of the award-winning *Divorce and Beyond Podcast*

"An illuminating, hopeful, and highly practical guide. Smolarski reframes co-parenting in the most empathic and eye-opening way, and gives parents a personal road map to a secure and healthy relationship with their kids and themselves. It's a must-read!"

—**Heather Turgeon**, psychotherapist, and coauthor of *The Happy Sleeper*

"My clients eventually realize that being a peaceful parent is not about our child—it's about managing ourselves. This is also true of co-parenting. Aurisha teaches us how to regulate ourselves, manage our own difficult feelings, and successfully navigate the co-parenting relationship while compassionately supporting our child so that they can flourish growing up in two households. I recommend this book for every parent of a child with two houses!"

—**Sarah Rosensweet**, peaceful parenting coach and educator; and host of the top-rated podcast, *The Peaceful Parenting Podcast*

To my daughter.
You inspire me to be the best mom
and co-parent I can be.

Contents

Foreword

When I was a young mom, I was a yeller, and I desperately needed some help. I was anxious, insecure, and struggling with a temper that seemed to rise up out of nowhere. It was an incredibly challenging situation, and I *wasn't* going through a separation at the time. Knowing how incredibly hard parenting is for all of us, I'm willing to bet that you may be going through a difficult time right now parenting through your separation. I imagine that, like me, you may be in need of wise counsel to help you understand yourself and your family members better, and help you navigate through these tricky waters.

Parenting is demanding under the best conditions, with the lack of sleep, the overwhelming responsibility, the noise, the mess, and the pushing of buttons that we didn't even know we had! There's pressure, joy, irritation, frustration, ambivalence (what did I get myself into?), play, and exhaustion all wrapped up in the experience of loving our children. It's stressful under optimal conditions, and when you add a divorce or separation into the parenting batter, you start to get worried about your muffins.

I turned to mindfulness to help me understand and tame my reactivity, so I could be the attuned, responsive parent I wanted to be. This book offers similar wise counsel and will help you develop awareness and understanding of your situation. How do you responsively co-parent with this person whom you *don't* want to spend time with? How do you communicate skillfully with your ex to raise your good human? Aurisha is an experienced, compassionate guide who walks you through this difficult transition, helping you feel seen and heard. As you move through the process laid out in this book, you will come to understand your own, your child's, and your co-parent's attachment style and how that affects each leg of your co-parenting journey. Through stories, science, and helpful dos and don'ts, you'll learn how to successfully collaborate on respectful parenting.

I teach mindful parenting, which is all about building awareness, understanding, and communicating skillfully. Without doing this awareness work, we're likely to repeat the same patterns that made everything so hard to begin with. We can't work with what we can't *see*, and I love the way Aurisha helps us see inner selves and habits from different perspectives, which is truly beneficial awareness. With the insights of attachment styles, you'll start to see where the bumps in the road will be, ahead of time, and plan accordingly. You'll understand why you react the way you do to things your parenting partner says. You'll be able to move beyond irritation and develop compassion and understanding so that you can both move forward constructively.

Thank you, Aurisha, for this book that helps us see and embrace all of our humanity, and raise good humans despite our gaffes and conflicts. Take your time and dive deep into this book. Do this important heart work now, and your whole family will benefit for years to come.

—Hunter Clarke-Fields, MSAE
Author of *Raising Good Humans*

Introduction

"Mommy…" My six-year-old daughter was sitting at the kitchen counter in her purple and blue flowered dress, her legs dangling from the wooden stool, her eyes cast toward the floor.

I knelt down in front of her, my eyes meeting hers. They were brimming with sadness, fear, and confusion. "Ellie, what's up, baby?"

"I feel all alone in the woods!" she cried.

I lifted up her head and held her face in my hands. My tears met hers. "I'm here with you, baby. I know everything feels confusing right now, but you're not alone."

I still remember my daughter's words as if she had uttered them yesterday. They were the wake-up call that torpedoed me out of my stupor about a week after Ellie's dad moved out of the house. They shook me to my core. The divorce I was going through was *my* nightmare; it shouldn't be hers!

Yet Ellie was suffering. She didn't feel secure. Her world had become full of unknowns, a scary "woods." We'd often taken walks in the woods together as a family, her dad and I holding her hands as we guided her along the winding rocky path. Now he wasn't here anymore. And I was too immersed in trying to keep my head above water to be fully present for her. Every day was a struggle to show up for my clients and to wrangle with the thoughts, anger, grief, anxiety, and fears that were trading places within my body and mind from moment to moment. No wonder Ellie felt lost!

Fortunately, I was able to hear her wake-up call. I took it to heart and used it to reshape the relationship I was embarking on: *co-parenting* with her dad. No matter how I felt about him, she needed the two of us to continue to provide safety, security, and clarity. I couldn't do that alone. Ellie needed her dad to be her dad, and I needed that too.

It was a humbling experience to sit at the intersection of my discomfort about relating to someone I never wanted to see again and my realization that healthy co-parenting was the best way to provide the comfort and secure base our daughter needed to thrive and grow. Her dad and I had made the choice to have a parenting partnership when we decided to have a child together. Now it was on us to differentiate the parenting part from the romantic part of our relationship, which was over. My daughter was asking us to continue being parents together, even under two roofs. It was up to us to listen and show up.

Our cultural understanding about how marriages and families should work has been and still is changing, especially in the United States. According to the Pew Research Center, about a quarter of US children under the age of eighteen live with one parent and no other adult; worldwide, single-parent homes are under 10 percent (Kramer 2019). Since the 1960s, family living arrangements have become more diverse (Pew Research Center 2015). More people are choosing to create different family systems, shifting away from the traditional paradigm of gender roles and structures. Some of this is related to the changing rates of divorce, remarriage, and nonmarital cohabitation.

You may be reading this because you are separated or divorced from a partner you previously parented with under one roof or because you've made a conscious choice to co-parent within some other arrangement. You may be a single parent or you may have partnered with someone else, or you may see co-parenting on your near horizon. You may have an infant or a toddler or a teen, or something in between. Whatever your unique situation, this book will guide you to create a co-parenting relationship that allows your child to thrive.

Beyond Separation and Divorce

Expectations for and dreams about a forever-intact family system are still largely upheld by mainstream culture. The sanctity of marriage with two parents living together is presumed as the ideal system for raising children in "till death do us part" promises. It is reflected in the Cinderella fairytale stories we read to our young kids and that they see on TV and in the movies they watch. The stigma of separation and divorce is still very real. Across many cultures, it creates narratives of shame, blame, failure, and threat. Even the labels "single mom" and "single dad" can set a tone of isolation and exclusion. They can cause a drastic change in your identity. You may feel you're now alone in parenting, an outcast from the way "it's supposed to be." You may notice some of your relationships changing, as people project their judgments or fears onto you and no longer show up for you in the same way.

I took on that shame narrative when I got divorced. I felt I'd failed because I couldn't keep our marriage together, that we'd failed as a couple because we couldn't do it for our child. But I also knew it was better for our daughter to see us happy apart than to see us slowly disintegrate into the depths of an "unhappy together" forever.

Sometimes it is better for the adults, and even for the children, if a nuclear family is dissolved and the parents live apart. As the adage goes, "A good divorce is better than a bad marriage." Research supports this. Child development expert Michael Lamb (2012) reported that children who grow up with the support and care of both parents—regardless of their family structure—adapt well to the changes, and they experience no lasting negative effects on their grades, ability to adapt in social situations and at school, and overall mental health. What matters is the involvement of a loving parent, not the living arrangements.

So, what might a good two-home family look like? For starters, the children would feel a sense of ease and stability. They would trust their parents to provide consistency and to be attuned to their emotional needs. They would feel seen and understood. They would see their parents interacting cordially. They would count on the protection, love, and support of their family. They would be free to be kids.

The breakup of a family is a major transition not only for adults but also for children. There are so many moving pieces, so many big emotions and stressors, and so many practical aspects and adjustments to figure out. It's a crisis with time pressure: you need to shift quickly into a new norm. The co-parenting relationship is as real and legitimate as a romantic partnership, and it deserves your utmost care and attention. Once your original family unit has broken, you can feel almost invisible in your struggles. If it weren't for the other single or co-parent moms I knew, I would have felt completely alone as I navigated this turn of events in my life.

After the wake-up call from my daughter, I realized I had a choice. I could choose to run with all my anger, resentment, and hurt, with the parts of myself that wanted to have a tantrum and yell at my ex, "This isn't fair" or "You hurt me, and I want revenge." Or I could remember that none of this was my daughter's fault and choose to put her needs front and center. Though I still felt deeply hurt and betrayed by my ex-husband, I could continue to develop the part of our relationship that hadn't ended: co-parenting. I decided to find a way to co-parent with my ex that was consistent with how I would have wanted to parent if we were still together—working as a team and being present as parents. What's more, I decided to do this even if my ex didn't commit to doing the same himself.

What Is Cooperative Co-Parenting?

Co-parenting is a legal and psychological term that refers to two parents jointly raising a child even though they are separated, divorced, or not living together. Although I'm talking primarily about separation and divorce, the principles in this book can be applied to a wide range of situations, including blended families and other alternative family arrangements.

In the UK, co-parenting is called *shared parenting*. I think this term captures the essence of cooperative co-parenting in a nutshell: you and your co-parent share the responsibility for care taking, decision-making, guidance, and being present for the emotional and physical needs of your child. You do this by working together and by communicating and coordinating routines and scheduling, so your child has consistency. You and your co-parent are considerate of each other, generous toward each other, and avoid talking negatively about each other in front of your child. You are committed to providing a secure environment for your child.

Cooperative co-parenting allows you to redesign a family system that still consists of two parents but now has two homes. The task is to realign yourselves, so you are on the same team—team kiddo. That team is organized around the goal of raising a healthy and confident child who, not burdened by separation and loss, enjoys learning, playing, and growing.

Co-parenting can feel pretty overwhelming at first. Parenting itself is hard. It's hard when you try to do it as a couple, and when you add a separation into the mix, it becomes even harder. You may think I'm being idealistic to suggest that, despite whatever caused your breakup, you and your ex-partner can function as an effective team. But you can! The key is realizing that your goal is no longer about the two of you succeeding; it's about your child succeeding. You're just working together to make sure that happens. As a result, you also succeed as parents. You don't have to like each other—although if you do, that helps. Rather, you have to understand your parental relationship and learn how to navigate each other within the new dynamic of co-parenting. In this book, I'm going to show you how to do that.

The Nuts and Bolts

Before we talk about how to co-parent effectively, let's look at three scenarios showing co-parents in the kinds of interactions every co-parent is familiar with. See if you can spot some critical differences between these scenarios.

- *Danica and Evan*

It's 7:20 a.m. and Danica is rushing around, getting ready for work, muttering annoyances about Evan. "I can't believe he's still not here. He has no respect for anyone. He knows I work Saturday mornings!" She lets out an exasperated sigh and turns to fourteen-year-old Kaley, "Honey, can you remind your dad to get here on time? He knows I can't be late to work."

Kaley rolls her eyes. "Yeah, Mom, whatever. I already told him. Maybe he's stuck in traffic." She walks outside and sits on the cement stairs, holding her backpack and listening to music on her headphones while she waits. When she finally sees her dad's car, she stands up to go.

Danica has been waiting too. She comes out and yells, "I'm so sick of you being late! I can't do everything, you know."

Evan raises his hand in a dismissive wave and yells back, "News flash! You're not my timekeeper anymore. So lay off!" He shakes his head as he remembers his upcoming business trip and thinks, No way am I dealing with that now. I'll tell her next week that she needs to take Kaley on Thursday.

"Hey, K baby," he says as his daughter gets in the car. "Sorry I'm late. You know how bad LA traffic is. Geez, your mom is so dramatic!"

Kaley doesn't respond. She puts on her seatbelt and looks out the window.

- *Olivia and Grace*

It's 7:00 a.m. and Olivia is getting ready for her Saturday shift at the hospital. She sees a text come in from her co-mom, Grace. "Ugh, looks like Mamma G will be twenty minutes late—again," she says to eight-year-old Mateo, who's playing a video game.

"Sure, Mom," he responds absently.

Olivia bustles about, putting dishes away. "Mateo, get off the screen," she barks. "I need you to be ready before Mamma G gets here."

"Let me finish my game," Mateo pleads.

"No! I can't have you being like Mamma G, always making me late!" Olivia shoots back. Immediately she regrets her words. "I'm sorry. But you're stressing me out. Can you please work with me, so we both get out of here in one piece?"

Mateo slams his computer shut and gets up to put his shoes on.

The doorbell rings. Mateo answers it, and Grace walks in. "Hey kiddo!" she says and kisses him on the cheek. "Oh, Olivia, I forgot to tell you I have a work trip next week. I can't pick Mateo up at school. Maybe he can stay with you, and I'll take him the following week?"

Olivia frowns. "If that's what you need, I'll figure it out. But you know, I also have a job."

Mateo looks worried as he glances between his moms.

• Regi and Leda

It's 9:00 a.m. Saturday, and Regi is rereading some emails he and Leda exchanged. He shoots off a text: "Sorry for the delay. I've been thinking about your upcoming trip. I can take Kevin. My neighbor will watch him while I finish at work. I do like the extra time with him but also need solo time. Let's coordinate to figure that out."

"Of course. Thanks for working with my schedule," Leda texts back. "This trip should guarantee my promotion."

Regi puts down his phone and turns to ten-year-old Kevin. "How about helping me wash these dishes?"

"Aww, Dad, do I have to?" Kevin complains but with a smile.

Regi and Kevin lose track of time and are just finishing their cleanup when Regi's text tone goes off. "What's your ETA?" the message reads.

"Oh geez, now we're running late!" Regi calls out. "Let's go!"
He sends a quick text to Leda letting her know they're on their way.

When they arrive, he apologizes for being late, and adds, "I won't make it a habit, promise!"

"It's okay." She gives him a half smile.

"Do you have a sec to tell him now?" Regi asks, as Kevin tumbles out of the car.

"Sure." Leda opens her arms as Kevin runs up to her. "Hi Kev! Can I give you a mama bear hug?" She laughs as he sheepishly submits. "Listen, your dad and I want to tell you about a little switcheroo next week. I have an important work trip, so you'll be staying at your home with Dad."

Kevin nods in agreement as Regi kisses his head and says, "I love you, buddy."

Did you see yourself in any of these scenarios? Let's take a closer look at each of them.

You probably noticed that Danica and Evan represent many things that can go wrong. They don't hold back when it comes to dishing out blame and arguing in front of their daughter. Kaley is bounced like a ball between them, absorbing all their conflict. Even something as seemingly minor as a twenty-minute delay becomes a major cause of friction. We can only imagine how they will handle talking about Evan's business trip, which he's left for a last-minute discussion.

In the second scenario, Olivia and Grace have managed to tame some of the hostility and resentment between them. Olivia has the self-awareness to apologize to Mateo after she lashes out at him. However, she doesn't refrain from saying negative things about her co-parent in front of him. The discussion of scheduling changes lacks clarity, and Olivia and Grace aren't on the same page in front of Mateo, leaving him confused and anxious.

Regi and Leda are our stellar example. They take the time and make the effort to communicate well between themselves, so when they're with their son, they have a united, harmonious presence. Kevin is happy and secure, knowing his two parents are working together to organize the details of his life, and feeling he can count on them to iron out any wrinkles (such as an unexpected business trip). Because his parents are clear with him, he can adapt well to the changes.

Your Co-Parenting Style

In and of itself, co-parenting is a neutral term. It simply means two parents are parenting the same child or children. It's how you do it that makes all the difference. This book will guide you to develop a style that works for you and your co-parent. It can be helpful to start with a sense of your current style. Here are twelve questions to consider.

1. Do the two of you always collaborate and cooperate to figure out changes in schedule?

2. Do you always communicate with clarity and share relevant information?

3. Do you always discuss changes before telling your kid?

4. Are you always considerate of each other's time and schedules?

5. Do you always present a unified front to your kid?

6. Do you always avoid criticizing, yelling, or throwing each other under the bus in front of your kid?

7. Do you always refrain from getting defensive or reactive when your co-parent makes a request?

8. Do you make good use of community or other external support systems when needed?

9. Do you always follow through on the agreements you and your co-parent establish?

10. Do you always maintain consistency in routines?

11. Do you always keep your kid from being a messenger between you and your co-parent?

12. Do you and your co-parent always make yourselves available to each other and to your kid?

If you answered yes to all twelve questions, you can probably breeze through this book. However, if you answered no to any or most of them, I think you'll find useful guidance to move you into a more effective style of co-parenting, even if it feels one-sided sometimes. It only takes one person to shift the dynamics in a relationship.

The Principles of Engagement

Co-parents who are struggling usually tell me something like this: "When I embarked on this journey, co-parenting felt overwhelming. I felt out of control every time I spoke with my ex. They'd say something, and I'd react emotionally. Then they reacted back. It was a never-ending cycle of shit we were throwing at each other. No one felt good."

You may know how co-parenting *should* look, but emotions get in the way. Anger, shame, resentments, blame, jealousy, and grief rule the show, and it can seem impossible to interact without getting caught in the line of reactionary fire.

I understand this because I've been there. Learning to co-parent with my daughter's dad was one of the most uncomfortable experiences I've ever had to sit with every day. We weren't together anymore, so it wasn't about being vulnerable with him. Rather, I had to be vulnerable with myself and learn to lean on my support system. I had to step out of my comfort zone, to let go of looking for acknowledgments I was never going to get from him. He was never going to understand my hurt or pain or needs in the way I wanted him to. This was, after all, in part why we were no longer together. As my friend and colleague Kara Hoppe once said when I was sharing my latest frustrations, "You were looking for roses in a hardware store." I was!

Ultimately, I was able to draw on my work as a psychotherapist, mediator, and public policy advocate and learn to be vulnerable in a new way. I was able to put down my weapon of anger and let go of my revenge fanta-sies as well as my desire to withhold, and meet my ex with openness and cordiality and a willingness to work together. This was best for my child and fundamentally also best for me.

Along the way, I came to understand and practice what I call the *principles of engagement* for successful co-parenting, or the six Cs of cooperative co-parenting:

Commitment: Co-parents create certainty in the midst of change by committing to show up and be present for their child, thereby creating trust and reducing anxiety.

Collaboration: Co-parents collaborate and work together with a shared vision for co-parenting to create win-wins for all.

Clarity: Co-parents maintain clear, concise, calm, and timely com-munications, thereby minimizing misunderstandings and providing accountability.

Consistency: Co-parents build consistent structures in both homes to create reliable and predictable environments.

Connection: Co-parents stay present and mindful with their child to help them process their emotions and to build secure attachment.

Community: Co-parents build community and support systems, thereby fostering a sense of belonging.

These principles are at the heart of any healthy co-parenting relation-ship. They set your family system up for success and healthy outcomes for all involved. I have found that when co-parents follow these principles, they also create a safe haven for their kids. It may take a while to establish what this looks like for your situation, but it is worth every bit of the work.

I didn't pull these six C words out of thin air. In fact, a wide range of experts have gathered lists of C words over the years, and many of their words overlap with mine. For example, lawyer Robin M. Mermans (2021) listed five Cs for co-parenting during the holidays. The six Cs comprising my principles of engagement are unique in that they represent my synthesis of how the principles of attachment theory relate to the co-parenting relationship.

Attachment theory, as originally described by John Bowlby (1969), is the primary theoretical orientation of this book. *Secure attachment* refers to the quality of the relationship between a parent and their child, whereby the child has a stable and secure basis from which to navigate life going forward. A child who has this kind of secure base can weather the storms of adversity—such as the changes that come with separation—much more easily than one who doesn't. Attachment patterns form in the first year of life but can change depending on the dynamics of the child's primary relationships. As a co-parent, understanding this offers a huge advantage. You and your co-parent can each learn to provide secure attachment for your child in your own homes, even though you are no longer all under the same roof. This, in a nutshell, is the key to overcoming the challenges of separation and creating an effective co-parenting relationship that allows your kid to thrive.

The Win-Win-Win

When co-parenting, you and your co-parent can decide to work for win-win-wins. You may be already familiar with the concept of a *win-win*, which means you don't have to settle for solutions in which one person wins and the other loses. Understanding your own and your co-parent's attachment styles will make this easier. As you learn to manage and soften your reactions, your interactions will become less conflictual. You will work together as a team and find a sense of mutuality. You'll start celebrating win-wins.

Your kid can't lose out either. When your co-parenting relationship is running like a well-oiled machine, you can focus on staying present and available to your kid and sensitive to their needs. This will decrease the traumatic impact of separation on them and increase the likelihood of them developing or maintaining a secure attachment style. Even if you are staring at pieces of your life strewn around or in a heap of mess, and feel overwhelmed and confused, with the help of this book you can start to reorganize and create a cooperative co-parenting structure that is a win-win-win—not just for you as co-parents but also for your child.

How to Use This Book

The initial chapters of this book give you the theoretical grounding you need to embark on your co-parenting journey. This is the introspective step that sets up your own personal win. You will learn how to identify your attachment style and that of your co-parent. You will work with and improve upon aspects of your style to better support secure attachment. I've included exercises and examples, so you can immediately put this understanding to use in your daily life.

While the focus of this book is on working cooperatively with your co-parent, what you bring to that relationship is critical. You've just gone through the trauma of a separation. It's only natural for your emotions to run high. Chapter 2 guides you in using the principles of secure attachment to deal with the sadness, anger, fear, and shame you may be feeling, so they don't get in the way of effective co-parenting. Chapter 3 completes this internal work—your individual win—with a deep dive into the ways you may react to your co-parent, including control-seeking behaviors, blame, and criticism.

The next chapters focus on the six Cs that comprise the principles of engagement for successful co-parenting. They show how each principle contributes to your ability to provide secure and effective co-parenting and to create win-wins with your co-parent. In these chapters, you will build a team with your co-parent. Each chapter includes tools and tips to guide you on this journey. The final chapter brings the power of the win-win-win into focus, as you launch your child into a world of security, love, and belonging.

This book is for you and your co-parent. But mostly, it is for *you*. Ideally, you and your co-parent will be on the same page when it comes to building your co-parenting partnership. But that may not be the case initially, and for some co-parents, it may never really be as much the case as you would wish. That's okay. I'm not asking you to change your co-parent. My ex and I didn't take this journey of becoming a co-parent team completely in tandem. Rather, by working on my own stuff and by better understanding his stuff, I was able to create the space we needed to move forward and continue to parent together. So let this book take you on a journey that begins with you, that invites your co-parent into cooperative partnership, and that continues regardless of your co-parent's choices. You will come away with a new level of control and new ways to lead, and with the satisfaction that you've done everything you possibly can to ensure a happy, secure, and wonderful life for your child.

Note that I sometimes use the term *ex* when referring to partners in the context of a prior romantic relationship. However, I highly suggest shifting away from calling your co-parent "my ex" to their face, in conversations about them, or even mentally to yourself. Instead, try claiming the label "my co-parent." It might sound insignificant, but the words we use carry power in our relationships.

As much as possible, I've written this book to be applicable for co-parents with kids of all ages and I've provided cases that span the infant through teen years. However, addressing specific age-related differences between infants and teens is beyond the scope of this book, so please choose those examples and exercises that are most relevant or make adjustments that best fit the developmental needs of your child.

Finally, this book is not meant to be a replacement for trauma therapy or other forms of professional support, either for you or for your kid. Separation and divorce are recognized as among the most prevalent adverse childhood experiences (ACE) that can have long-lasting negative effects if not treated (Sacks and Murphey 2018). Co-parenting can trigger memories of old trauma or attachment wounding. You may also encounter problems such as high-conflict interactions and abusive or unsafe behavior. If any of this is the case for you, please seek the professional guidance you need.

Chapter 1

Your Attachment Cables

Do any of these comments sound familiar?

"It's like the relationship never happened, like he's suddenly forgotten we were ever a couple!"

"She knows I'm busy. I'll get back to her when I can. Not sure why she gets so upset!"

"Ugh, I don't know why I still look at his social media every day. I mean, we're over, and I don't care if he's dating!"

"I'm fine on my own. I just wish he could be more self-sufficient too."

"Every time I say something, he gets so defensive. I'm just trying to share info."

"I'm sure her new boyfriend will see soon enough how selfish she is. I hope he dumps her!"

"She's so demanding. She can't put that stuff on me."

"If only I had…maybe we'd still be together."

These comments reflect patterns of behavior or reactions and thoughts that are common among newly separated co-parents. I listed them because they can also be indicative of your attachment style. As you read this chapter, you'll be able to come back to these comments and recognize which styles they represent. Perhaps more importantly, you will understand your attachment style and what it means for your co-parenting relationship.

As discussed in the introduction, *attachment* refers to the relationship between caregiver and child that influences the child's development and how they view themself in the world. Your early attachment, in turn, influences both how you relate to another adult—whether that's your partner or, in this case, your ex-partner—and to your own child. In this and the next chapter, you will do some introspective work to lay a foundation for building a cooperative team with your co-parent.

Let's start by looking in greater depth at the principles of attachment theory and how they play out in the context of co-parenting. I'm going to introduce you to the three main styles of attachment. After that, you will have a chance to get a sense of what your own style is as well as that of your co-parent. We will conclude by looking at your kid's attachment style. I'll describe how to spot any issues related to attachment that may be exacerbated by separation and divorce and how to make sure your child feels securely attached.

The Basics of Attachment Theory

We all have an attachment style that we bring into our relationships. Our style plays out in daily interactions through common patterns of behavior, especially when we're under stress. We developed our attachment style during our early childhood, in response to the ways our caregivers—that is, our initial attachment figures—responded or didn't respond to our needs when we were experiencing stress, fear, disappointment, or separation. We were all born with a biological drive to seek protection and closeness from a caregiver. We relied on our primary caregiver to be present and sensitive to our signals for connection and to provide us with a consistent and secure base—that is, with *secure attachment*. Once these needs were met, we could move on from any momentary crisis and resume a state of calm and ease. We could go back to playing, learning, and exploring the world, knowing we were secure. We developed the confidence that we were safe and loved.

Not all of us had parents who were able to provide secure attachment. Parents who aren't predictably responsive and attuned to their child display what we call *insecure attachment*. If you experienced insecure parenting as a child, you know it feels like a lonely or scary place. You may have had to develop adaptive strategies to ensure your survival. In fact, the feelings, expectations, and behaviors that form our attachment style start as early as nine to twelve months and stick with us throughout our lives as we navigate relationships at home, at work, and with friends. Our attachment style shows up in how we choose partners; how we try to get our emotional needs met; and how we deal with intimacy, conflict, separations, and loss. When we enter into romantic relationships, our partners become our new attachment figures. When we become parents, we become attachment figures for our kids.

Drawing on the theory first formulated by John Bowlby (1969), Mary Ainsworth and her colleagues (1978) identified three main attachment styles: avoidant, ambivalent, and secure. These styles are based on the responses Ainsworth observed when children experienced their mother leaving a room briefly and then returning. The securely attached children got distressed by the separation but were easily soothed upon their mother's return. The avoidantly attached children showed no outwardly visible distress during the separation but avoided or ignored their mother upon her return. The ambivalently attached children were highly distressed by the separation and, upon their mother's return, were hard to sooth, displaying both anger and a desire for close contact. Subsequent studies with fathers found similar outcomes. More recently, psychologists such as Stan Tatkin (2012) and Sue Johnson (2013) have written about how these attachment behaviors are reflected in adult romantic relationships. Here we'll discuss how they show up in the co-parenting relationship too.

It's estimated that 50 to 60 percent of adults have secure attachment, with the remainder split fairly evenly between avoidant and ambivalent attachment (Levine and Heller 2010). Your attachment style doesn't make you a good or a bad person. Each style holds its own superpowers and struggles. Even with secure attachment, problems do come up. Nor are our styles fixed. Rather, they exist on a continuum, and we can move from one style to another at different phases and in different situations and relationships in our lives. For example, you may shift toward insecure attachment in a stressful relationship or toward secure attachment as you better understand your past experiences.

Each of us comes into our adult relationships carrying our own internal map, including attachment patterns we may be unaware of; not to mention, we're likely unaware of our partner's attachment history. However, both partners recognize when someone steps on their landmines. For this reason, it's helpful to understand how attachment works, so you can learn to read the signs and navigate each other's map.

Invisible Cables

What does all this mean when you separate or divorce and kids are involved? Separations send our attachment system into high gear, much as we saw in Ainsworth's experiment. They create new stress, amplify existing or past stress, and undermine our feelings of security. There you are, suddenly faced with a permanent separation from your partner, who until very recently was your attachment person. To make things more complicated, when kids are in the mix, it's not really permanent, because your ex is still in your life. Now you have to untangle yourself from them while at the same time maintaining a relationship as co-parents. Goodbye…but not quite. Talk about confusing!

Even if you and your ex weren't good at soothing each other or providing the care and reliability you needed while together, you were wired such that you went to each other for security, to be each other's safe haven. Whether it was effective or not, you were part of a joint system of attachment. I like to use the analogy of invisible cables. For better or for worse, your cables were plugged into each other, and the two of you are likely still plugged in, in some ways. Now you have to unplug, and fast! Your frayed cables are flailing in the wind, in all their glory and confusion.

The ways you and your ex are behaving in response to separation, to the unplugging of your cables, didn't just start with your breakup or divorce. It started in the murky waters of the past and the development of your respective attachment styles. The good news is that learning about this aspect of yourself gives you a clear path back to secure attachment. When I understood my attachment style and that of my ex, I was able to see how we were triggering each other. I better understood why he reacted to my requests the way he did. I also saw why I kept seeking his acknowledgment. With this awareness, I was able to shift how I approached him. I was able to stop trying to get something from him that was no longer his to give me. As we both became less reactionary, our interactions as co-parents became calmer and less conflicted.

Let's take a look at the three attachment styles, so you can learn more about yourself and your co-parent. This will empower you to shift old patterns and learn healthier ways to navigate your co-parenting relationship. It will also help you as a parent. In the introduction, you met three sets of co-parents who were dealing with a Saturday changeover. I'll include these co-parents' backstories here to show how different attachment styles function within a co-parenting relationship.

Avoidant Attachment

People with avoidant attachment have an independent streak. Their superpowers include being creative, persistent, and invested in and focused on their professional development. They go through life with the attitude "when things are hard, put your head down and move on." While they may take pride in being low-maintenance and self-sufficient, their struggles come from an emotional landscape that can be sparse and lonely. While they may *want* connection, they keep others at a safe distance.

As kids, those with avoidant attachment had a primary caregiver who, even if physically present, was distant and not emotionally attuned to their child's distress signals. As babies, their cries for comfort were dismissed or ignored. From their early experiences, these kids learned to control their emotions because they couldn't count on their caregivers to meet their needs; they had to rely on themselves. Because they were often neglected, they learned to feel seen and loved through meeting the expectations of others. They had to work hard to maintain the perception of having it all together.

As adults, these individuals seek out and thrive in situations where they can work alone and their autonomy is honored. Collaboration and team building don't come easily. They may see love as performance- and achievement-based. In relationships, intimacy is scary because it can threaten their safety and independence, so they find ways to maintain their sense of freedom. They can be very private, keep secrets, withdraw from closeness, and sometimes have affairs. Some people with avoidant attachment can be overly focused on their own needs and desires; others may not express their needs and emotions at all. These distancing behaviors are a means of keeping the peace and avoiding the pain of rejection. When conflict does arise and a partner with avoidant attachment perceives criticism or judgment, they will likely shut down emotionally or be the first one out the door.

Being or doing something wrong means *I am bad* or *I'm invisible*, which can feel unsafe and scary and lead to defensiveness. They try to caretake their partner as a way to feel worthy, even without truly connecting. People with avoidant attachment may be viewed as closed off and rigid. Their dismissive behavior of "I don't need you. I'm fine on my own" can be perceived as controlling or ignoring, but really they're saying "Please, please, tell me I'm good enough!"

- ### *Evan's Story*

  As a video editor, Evan relishes his alone time. In his relationship with Danica, he often felt suffocated by what he saw as her demands for closeness and affection. He was never able to be fully present with her, but he was okay with that.

Evan's avoidant attachment can be traced to his parents. Although both loved Evan, neither was fully present for him when he was young. His father traveled for work and often came home late, tired, and in a foul mood. His mother juggled her time between working in a daycare center, keeping up with Evan's brother, who was always getting into trouble, and taking classes toward a college degree. As a result, she was often stressed and irritable and didn't have much time for Evan.

Evan learned early that crying wouldn't get him anywhere except a trip to his room to "buck up and get over it." As he got older, Evan learned to stay out of the way and would stay in his bedroom, playing video games, drawing, or getting lost in a movie. Evan would heat up leftovers for himself and his brother and got used to going to bed on his own. At the same time, Evan looked up to his father and sought his approval. His dad's silent look of disappointment when Evan didn't get all As stung to the core. Evan did everything he could to be seen as a perfect son. That meant he was worthy.

AVOIDANT ATTACHMENT AND BREAKUPS

Because a breakup can cause shame or fear of failure, people with avoidant attachment will do what they can to minimize engagement with their exes. Their tendency to dismiss their own feelings and those of their partners can be even more evident after a breakup. It's as if their attachment cables were already loose, and they just want to shake themselves free. They cope with the grief and pain of separation by distancing themselves and shutting down emotionally. They find it hard to apologize and may tell themselves the relationship was doomed to fail.

Initially, they may appear fine and unaffected by the breakup, as they go about focusing on their job and settling into an independent life. This gives them confidence and a sense of feeling under control. However, their old rejection wounds and lowered self-worth are likely to creep in pretty quickly. They may jump into a new relationship or a series of short rebound relationships and continue to suppress feelings associated with the separation. Over the longer term, their emotional cave gets full, and they may start to experience increased mental and physical distress, such as anxiety and depression.

In the introduction, you saw Evan display some of these avoidant behaviors. He doesn't communicate to Danica when he is running late. He dismisses her complaint when he arrives, and he avoids talking with her about his upcoming trip because it's easier to stay silent. Evan is sensitive to Danica's critical comments and typically walks away from her or doesn't respond. But the old nagging voice of shame from his childhood whispers deep inside that maybe he still isn't good enough. Sometimes—as in our Saturday morning scenario—his sensitivity to criticism leads him to become defensive and, instead of withdrawing, to turn the blame on Danica: he does this by complaining to Kaley that her mom is "so dramatic." At the end, we see Kaley distancing herself from the parental conflict by seeking refuge in her music and not responding, which suggests she may be well on the way to developing her own avoidant style.

Ambivalent Attachment

People with ambivalent attachment love to communicate and maintain closeness and connection. Their superpowers include being flexible, accommodating, and highly devoted in relationships. They're good at prioritizing the needs of others and work well in collaborative settings. However, even though they surround themselves with people, they don't feel they can completely count on those relationships. Their struggle comes from the desire to be loved, while waiting for the proverbial other shoe to drop when they are left.

People with ambivalent attachment had caregivers who either were inconsistently available (sometimes present and sometimes not) or had emotional states that intruded on the child's inner world. Even if physically present, the parent may have been too preoccupied with their own needs and emotions to be sensitive to their child, leaving the child unsure about if and how their caregiver would show up. As a result, the child had to develop strategies to maintain closeness. They may have minimized their own feelings as a way to keep their parent from getting upset, or they may have put their feelings on blast to elicit a response. Either way, their sense of self was fraught with confusion and uncertainty.

In adult relationships, those with ambivalent attachment yearn to be seen and understood and may feel preoccupied with unresolved issues from the past. They seem to have an insatiable need for closeness yet struggle to fully trust their partners. This is the paradox of ambivalent attachment: the person wants love, but they are so afraid of losing that love that they are always scanning for signs of abandonment or rejection. They may try to control their environment as a way of keeping their partner close and creating the semblance of reliable love. Attempts to elevate their partner's needs over their own often lead to resentment or anger. They aren't skilled at expressing their needs directly, so they try indirect strategies, sometimes pushing their partner away when what they really want is for their partner to come closer. This push-pull behavior can be perceived as possessive, clingy, or needy, but really they're just saying "Please, please tell me I'm lovable and you'll always be there for me!"

• Olivia's Story

Olivia is a nurse and gets a lot of recognition at work for going above and beyond. Even so, she often feels overwhelmed, afraid she can't keep up and will lose her job. The same was true in her relationship with Grace. Whenever she had to work late, she worried Grace would turn to a friend and end up leaving her for good.

Olivia's parents split when she was seven. She saw her dad on weekends, but he was depressed. He drank more openly after the breakup, and was not very engaged with her. Olivia knew it made him happy to hear about her good grades. She enjoyed their ice cream outings whenever she got her report card.

Olivia's mom worked hard to buy a house in an upscale neighborhood and cared a lot about appearances. As a youngster, Olivia did everything possible to please her mom. She wanted to avoid the cold front she would get if she didn't dress or act the way her mom wanted. She eventually learned that serving her mom breakfast in bed helped warm her up. As a teenager, Olivia didn't feel safe coming out to her mom. She didn't trust her mother to accept her for who she was. Instead, she felt she had to fit the mold of how she was supposed to behave if she wanted to be loved. Trying to argue with her mom was futile.

AMBIVALENT ATTACHMENT AND BREAKUPS

People with ambivalent attachment are not fans of being alone. They will cling a bit too long to a relationship, even if it has become toxic. It's like their cables are strung super tight, and they don't want to let go. Unlike people with avoidant attachment tendencies, those with ambivalent attachment exhibit obvious signs of emotional turmoil, anger, or distress. They find it hard to calm themselves, and old abandonment wounds and fears of never finding love creep in. They can also become preoccupied with their ex: they may try to punish them, have revenge fantasies, follow their every move on social media, or pump their child for info. They may long for the old relationship or try to reconcile with their ex. They may also keep seeking connection through text, email, phone, or even flirtation.

Looking back at Olivia, you can see some of these ambivalent tendencies in her interactions with Grace. The dynamic between them is strained. Instead of expressing her true feelings, Olivia accommodates Grace's last-minute request for her to keep Mateo the following week, even though doing so puts more of a burden on herself. She is unaware that she is still in the habit of trying to please her co-parent. Olivia's need for connection also comes through the number of texts she sends to Grace. Gaining info feels soothing to her and serves as a way to keep their family intact, even though she and Grace are no longer together. This tension spills over into her interactions with their son, Mateo. She blames him for her own stress and tries to lure him into taking her side against Grace. Mateo is used to being caught in the middle between his moms. One of his coping strategies is keeping his nose in a video game.

Secure Attachment

People with secure attachment have confidence and self-esteem. They are open, warm, trusting, and emotionally present and adapt well under stress. With these superpowers, they maintain healthy relationships at home, with friends, and at work. They're easy to like. They don't have serious internal conflicts, as those with avoidant or ambivalent attachment do. They know they are worthy of love, and whenever an issue does surface, they know how to communicate and get their needs met.

Securely attached kids grew up with a caregiver who was consistent, present, and responsive to their emotional needs. Their parents were affectionate, took genuine interest in their child's emotional world, and repaired any ruptures quickly, without shame or blame. Secure kids knew they could rely on their parent to unconditionally cherish and protect them.

As adults, those who are securely attached bring that felt sense of security and open communication into relationships. They can embrace intimacy with a partner without losing their sense of self; they can hold on to the "I" within the "we." Like everyone else, they encounter relationship issues, loss, disappointments, and emotional ups and downs. However, their secure attachment allows them to maintain emotional balance as they tumble through the messy and complicated aspects of relationships. They can manage their emotional reactions, can repair misunderstandings before things escalate, and are quick to forgive.

● *Regi's Story*

Regi works at a convenience store and manages an art studio on weekends. He is easygoing and has a rich social life and a busy workload, but also always prioritizes time with his son.

Regi's parents were divorced but were emotionally present on the days they had their kids. Regi remembers his mother tenderly wiping his tears when he fell off a swing at the playground. They maintained some shared family moments in their respective homes, such as each talking about the ups and downs of their day at dinnertime, which created a sense of continuity and security.

Regi felt seen and understood. When he didn't make the basketball team, his dad sat with him over hot cocoa to acknowledge Regi's disappointment and shared his own story about not getting a job he wanted. His mom often rushed out the door in a flurry, but she never forgot to kiss and hug her kids as she left. She got annoyed at times when they did not clean their rooms, but she apologized for sounding snappy and tried to work out a solution with them. Regi's parents may not have both been securely attached, but after the breakup, they provided a secure environment in both his homes.

SECURE ATTACHMENT AND BREAKUPS

Those who are securely attached can acknowledge when it's time to end a relationship, and they don't take it as a personal failure or as proof they are unlovable. They feel the emotions that normally follow a separation or loss, but they know how to sit with their discomfort and how to reach out for support from nonromantic relationships and other resources. Their attachment cables are flexible and can stretch to fit their new co-parenting relationship. They work through the separation with acceptance and resilience and may use it as an opportunity for self-growth. They can examine how they both contributed to the separation and work with their ex toward an amicable ending. They know that fundamentally they will be okay.

Regi manages the morning changeover with ease and apologizes when he's running late. He's flexible when Leda requests a schedule change, while he also expresses his own needs and boundaries. He makes sure they are on the same page before letting their son know about the change, thus operating as a united front. Their interaction is cordial and calm; they stay present with Kevin and provide him with a friendly and warm transition. Kevin is at ease and feels free to enjoy the tenderness of both parents.

Identify Your Attachment Style

Read the following statements, which exemplify the different attachment styles. Choose the ones that most represent your own thoughts and feelings, and write them in your journal. It's fine to identify with statements under more than one attachment style. Note that while this exercise is not a diagnostic tool, it is designed to give you a better sense of which style you may tend toward.

Examples of avoidant attachment:

- *I enjoy my alone time.*

- *When I need something, I rely on myself to take care of it.*

- *I'd rather think things through on my own than communicate with others.*

- *Opening up to others and asking for help makes me uncomfortable.*

- *My ex wanted things from me that I couldn't give.*

- *If my co-parent upsets me, I have to go off by myself to calm down.*

- *I'm self-reliant and don't need to talk things over with my co-parent.*

- *Rules are rules, and compromise may mean I'm being taken advantage of.*

- *I hate the feeling that my co-parent still depends on me.*

- *Being wrong makes me feel unsafe or like I am bad.*

Examples of ambivalent attachment:

- *I thrive in the company of others.*

- *Separations scare me because I feel I may never find love again.*

- *I get frustrated if other people are unavailable when I need them.*

- *Others don't care about me as much as I care about them.*

- *It's hard for me to completely trust other people.*

- *I tend to say things that I later regret.*

- *I was always giving and giving to my ex and not getting as much in return.*

- *I think about my co-parent a lot, and I still seek approval from them.*

- *If my co-parent upsets me, I need to work it out immediately.*

- *I'm still mad at my co-parent and will always be.*

Examples of secure attachment:

- *I value a balance between being with others and having alone time.*

- *When situations change, I adapt quickly.*

- *I know I will be okay after a separation.*

- *It is easy for me to depend on others for support.*

- *Even though we're not together, I appreciate my co-parent.*

- *I am supportive and friendly with my co-parent.*

- *I discuss my concerns with my co-parent directly.*

- *If my co-parent upsets me, I stay calm and don't escalate the situation.*

- *I am willing to work on a win-win.*

- *Prioritizing the agreements with my co-parent is important to me.*

Now look at which statements you chose. Do you notice any patterns? If you chose more statements under one attachment style, that is likely to be your style. If you don't see a clear pattern, this may be a time in your life when you are fluctuating between different styles. Remember that attachment styles can change, especially in times of stress.

Now go through the list again, this time noting the statements that reflect your co-parent's thoughts and feelings. Alternatively, if you and your co-parent are relating in a manner that supports this kind of inter-action, you may invite them to do this exercise on their own. Either way, see if you can get a sense of your respective attachment styles. This awareness will be helpful as you work through the following chapters.

Finally, take a moment to reflect on the following questions:

- *What are my personal attachment style superpowers?*

- *What struggles come from my attachment style?*

- *What specific attachment style behaviors would I like to change?*

- *What are my co-parent's attachment style superpowers?*

- *What struggles come from my co-parent's attachment style?*

Being aware of your style and your partner's style will help you move toward more secure attachment in your role as co-parents.

Now that you're becoming familiar with attachment styles, you can apply this awareness to your child.

Tracking Your Child's Style

Researchers have found that a child's attachment style typically reflects that of their parents and the environment they grow up in (Siegel and Bryson 2020). Additionally, a child may develop different attachment pat-terns with each parent in response to how their parents show up for them. In a separated household, this may become more apparent, with a child being securely attached to one parent while exhibiting insecure attach-ment patterns with the other. The good news is that you and your co-parent can change the narrative. Attachment styles are not set in stone, and just as you can work on understanding your own patterns of attachment and where they came from, you can do a lot to help your child feel secure with you and in their world.

For starters, let's look at how different styles of attachment tend to show up in the behavior of children and adolescents. From here you can learn to track your kid's attachment style.

Child or Adolescent with Avoidant Attachment

A child with avoidant attachment won't seek comfort or contact from their caregiver. Instead, they show premature signs of independence. They are emotionally distant, sometimes to the point of not reacting differently to a caregiver and a stranger. They are wary of physical affection, such as hugs and kisses. They prefer to play alone and with objects rather than with other kids.

Teens with avoidant attachment may have low self-esteem and be dismissive or defiant. They can become defensive and be suspicious of empathic gestures from a teacher or a counselor and retreat from offers of support. They have few friends, preferring to be on their own, and their peers may perceive them as controlling. They may turn toward coping strategies such as social media, substance abuse, cutting, suicidality, or eating disorders and may show signs of depression or anxiety. Even if they look like they're fine, they are likely feeling anxious and stressed on the inside.

Child or Adolescent with Ambivalent Attachment

A child with ambivalent attachment tends to be anxious and struggles to cope with their emotions. At an early age, they may be inconsolable when a caregiver leaves; they can't be easily comforted and may become angry when reunited. They cling and stay close to their parent instead of exploring their environment with their peers. They are fearful of strangers and show signs of aggressive behavior or hyperactivity.

Teens with ambivalent attachment may have low self-esteem and exhibit erratic and aggressive emotions. Because they crave acceptance from their peers, they may become jealous and overly dependent on friends for their self-worth. They may turn to coping strategies such as social media, eating disorders, substance use, promiscuity, cutting, and suicidality instead of reaching out for help. They may show signs of depression or anxiety. Unlike teens with avoidant attachment, they tend to respond positively to attention from teachers or counselors.

Child or Adolescent with Secure Attachment

A child with secure attachment has a normal range of age-appropriate emotions. They seek comfort from their caregiver and are easily comforted. They are trusting, happy, and feel safe to explore their world while testing the limits of their independence. They prefer their parents to strangers but can separate from their parents with ease and are always happy to see them when they reunite.

Secure teens no longer rely solely on their parents but turn toward friends, teachers, and supportive adults. Even so, they gain confidence knowing their parents are supportive and present. They are socially engaged, creative, and able to take in new experiences and learning. They tend to be well-adjusted and balanced and cope well with the realities and emotional roller coaster of being a teen.

Observing Your Child

This exercise will help you get a sense of your child's attachment style. This isn't about making a diagnosis or placing a label on your child. Rather, it's a chance to become more familiar with specific behaviors your child engages in that may or may not support their development. First read through the examples of behaviors that fall under each attachment style. I've pared down these lists to describe kids over a range of different ages (over the age of two).

Examples of avoidant behaviors:

- Has few friends, spends a lot of alone time in their room

- Doesn't seek physical affection from you

- Is defiant at school

- Says, "I'm fine," retreats, or sulks when asked about their feelings

- Doesn't ask for help

- Is guarded around supportive adults

Examples of ambivalent behaviors:

- Is overly clingy and stays close to you or other adults

- Cries excessively during transitions

- Displays angry or aggressive behavior at school

- Has tantrums beyond the appropriate age and is not easily soothed

- Is frequently anxious about what their friends think of them

- Seeks attention from adults; is the class clown

Examples of secure behaviors:

- Makes friends easily; can share and collaborate

- Seeks out and enjoys affection

- Reengages easily with you after a separation

- Asks for help directly; accepts direction and guidance

- Talks openly about feelings and experiences

- Is confident, trusting; adapts well to new situations

Now observe your child over the next week or two, and see if you recognize any of these behaviors in them. You may need to adapt the descriptions; for example, if your child is younger, you can substitute "day care" for "school." If you have more than one child, you may want to observe them on different weeks. You will be observing your child while they are in your care; however, feel free to seek observations from your co-parent as well, if that feels comfortable.

At the end of the observation period, check the lists of behaviors described here. Did you notice behaviors that fall into any of the styles?

Attachment styles fall on a continuum, so don't be concerned if your child's behaviors indicate more than one style. Remember that attachment styles continue to evolve beyond early childhood, during the formative years of adolescence, and later. Furthermore, your child may have different attachment behaviors when they are with you than when they are with their other parent. In the following chapters, you will learn a variety of ways to increase your parental sensitivity and attunement so you can make a positive impact on your child's future.

● ● Now What? ● ●

As we conclude each chapter, I'll close with some questions I hear frequently and that you may have as you start doing the inner work around attachment styles.

Question: "Learning that I'm far from having secure attachment makes me feel anxious. What can I do about that?"

Answer: Keep in mind that stressful situations—such as a new separation—can push you along the attachment continuum. They can bring out your avoidant or ambivalent tendencies. See if you can recognize that and hang with it for now. Just becoming aware of where you are and what you're feeling is an important first step. As you read on, you will learn ways to move toward secure attachment.

Question: "My co-parent has avoidant attachment. What if he is hostile to participating in this or other exercises?"

Answer: While it's ideal for co-parents to collaborate as much as possible, you don't need your co-parent's involvement to create a positive home environment for your child. Research has shown that children can develop secure attachment even with one parent (Siegel and Bryson 2020). So, first and foremost, focus on your own relationship with your child.

Question: "My daughter often clings to my co-parent. He seems to like it. Should I tell him he's messing things up?"

Answer: It's great you can observe some of your daughter's attachment behaviors and how they play out with your co-parent. Approaching it as problematic won't help him or your kid. I suggest first working with the principles of engagement in the next chapter. This will help you find effective ways to communicate and be curious about what may be going on and how to better support your child.

Chapter 2

Untangling Your Emotional Cables

On so many of those first nights after separating from my partner, instead of falling into the welcome quiet of sleep, I found myself curling up in a ball under the sheets, sobbing. I felt unanchored, adrift in a sea of thoughts fueled by sadness, anger, and fear. I was sad seeing the life I had set up suddenly crumble. It was as if all our smiles had been smeared away and all I could feel were clenched fists of rage and disappointment. I was angry I hadn't been able to change my partner or fix our relationship. Fear held my stomach in knots as I wondered, *What's next? Who am I now? What will people think of me?* Shame crept in with the fear that I wasn't good enough, that I had failed myself and my daughter.

Eventually, I learned to sit in the vulnerability of my emotions. I had to dig deep into the trenches of my inner world to show up as the co-parent I wanted to be. I needed to focus on myself, the only person I had control over. The first step was recognizing that I was grieving a loss. Grief is like a vessel that holds a multitude of emotions in response to loss. Each of us cycles through these emotions at our own pace, and one or another feeling can become dominant at any given time.

Your emotions can make it hard to detach from your co-parent. A whole set of attachment and emotional cables keep you two wired together. You might think you need all those cables to power your life and feel okay. But what you really want is to be able to untangle them, so you can plug back into yourself. Then, if and when you decide to connect with a new partner, you will know how to remain plugged into yourself while connecting with someone else.

In this chapter, we will look at how the main emotional protagonists—sadness, anger, fear, and shame—can manifest after a breakup. I chose these four emotions because they're the ones that show up most consistently in the co-parents I work with. When left unprocessed, they can keep you stuck, contribute to conflict, and lead to longer-term grief and unhealed trauma. We will look at how each of these emotions feels in your body, the kinds of thoughts and beliefs associated with it, and what happens when you are triggered. We'll also discuss how these emotions are related to your attachment style. Finally, I will give you a process to start untangling your emotional cables from your co-parent and plugging them back into yourself. Understanding your emotions and where they come from isn't about making feelings disappear; it's about learning to navigate your inner world—your "stuff"—so you can develop successful relationships with your co-parent and your kids. Let's start with sadness.

Sadness

Tears are streaming down Cameron's cheeks as he stands next to his co-parent's car, cradling their baby in his arms. "I guess there's nothing more I can do to make this work," he says. "And you don't love me—us—enough to even try."

Jason opens the car door and sits in the driver's seat. "It's not that I don't love you. Or that I'm not sad. And you know how much I love Robbie! It's just that I can't keep doing this. I know it's hurting you, but I have to take care of myself."

"Yeah, in your new apartment." Cameron chokes back a sob. "With your new things and your new boyfriend."

Jason stares at the steering wheel. "Stop acting like it's all my fault. Like I said, I'm trying to deal. I can't be crying all day."

Sadness is one of the core emotions, an emotion all of us have probably felt to one degree or another. It is an experience of being unhappy. It can be associated with grief, loss, despair, or disappointment. When a relationship ends, it is normal to feel sadness. You're mourning the loss of an intimate connection that had held so much hope at one point. You may express your sadness overtly (like Cameron) or keep it hidden (like Jason).

Your sadness likely is associated with feelings of loss, hurt, or being abandoned. You may feel sad that you weren't or aren't loved or understood in the way you needed. Or you may feel sad because you've lost an important relationship that was part of your identity. You may miss or long for your ex and the routines you created in the relationship. And, of course, you may feel sad because you will no longer see your kids every day. When you're sad, you may feel less motivated to participate in your normal routines or social activities. It may be harder to complete tasks or stay present with your kids. Eating or drinking patterns may become less healthy.

Researchers from the University of Texas who studied people feeling sad found that changes in their brains led to an increased release of inflammatory proteins in their blood (Prossin et al. 2016). This, in turn, increased their risk for heart disease and stroke. Unprocessed sadness can lead to depression, which further increases these risks. Fortunately, sadness usually dissipates as time passes after a breakup. If you are feeling sad, I encourage you to find support from a friend or even a professional if you feel you need it, so you don't have to process your sadness alone and so it doesn't become entrenched.

You can feel sadness in the body as well as in the mind, and your attachment style will influence your experience of sadness.

Sadness in the Body

Sadness, like all emotions, can be a full body experience. Crying is one clear indication of sadness, but you can feel sad without shedding any tears. Many men, in particular, have been socialized to believe they should avoid crying or other expressions of sadness. When you're sad, the corners of your lips may droop, and your eyes may dim. Your body may feel heavy or achy, and you may notice tightness or heaviness in your chest. You may experience headaches, especially if you are unable to express your sadness through crying. Some people have less energy and want to sleep more when they're sad; others experience insomnia.

Sadness in the Mind

The following are common thoughts and beliefs associated with sadness after a breakup:

This hurts so much.

I'll miss my kid and their special moments.

I feel alone and lost.

I feel hopeless.

My dreams are over.

It's hard to wake up and get through the day.

Nothing can make me feel better.

Notice if you have any of these or similar thoughts associated with sadness. For now, I'm not asking you to do anything with them; just become aware of how sadness can manifest in your mind.

Sadness and Attachment

How your early caregivers responded to your expressions of sadness will affect how you manage sadness as an adult. Now that you've started to get a sense of your attachment style, you can further hone that understanding by considering how sadness was handled in your early life and how you handle it now.

If you resonate with secure attachment, your caregivers likely met your sadness with comfort and understanding. You grew up feeling your sadness had intrinsic value, because your caregivers made it clear they valued everything about you. Now you may reach out to friends and family for comfort when you feel sad, but you're also able to manage your own sadness. You don't let it spill over into your relationships with your co-parent and child. You accept the sadness that comes with a breakup, without letting it overwhelm you.

If you have avoidant attachment, you probably related to Jason's way of dealing with sadness. Most likely your early caregivers didn't allow much room for your sadness. They dismissed or minimized it. They may even have ridiculed or punished you for crying. Now you may not always realize when you're sad or accept that you feel sad. Instead, you may feel numb. Or if you feel a hint of sadness, you may quickly dismiss or shut it down. Isolating or reaching for new relationships or drugs and alcohol are common ways people avoid feeling sadness.

If you have ambivalent attachment, you wear your emotions on your sleeve, like Cameron. Your sadness may take priority in your life for a while. How your sadness was met when you were a child depended on the passing moods of your caregivers. Your caregivers may have been too self-absorbed when you were sad to make space for your feelings, or perhaps they made your sadness all about them. For example, if you appeared sad when a parent didn't attend your school event, they might have shifted your focus to whatever was wrong in *their* life that caused them to miss it. When you felt sad, you likely exaggerated your expression of it to get a response. Now you have difficulty managing your sadness on your own and may rely on others to help you feel better. Looking to your co-parent for consolation may be a sign your emotional cables are still plugged into them.

Fear

The emotion of fear may not be as visible as sadness, but it can keep you unable to be fully present with yourself and others. Here's a scenario in which fear plays a leading role.

"I'm going to go broke paying for two homes as well as child support," Tom wails. "And now you're saying you won't let me see Lizzie unless I pay more?"

Melissa feels her breath tighten in her chest. "Come on, you can afford it. Didn't you just get a promotion?"

"Yeah…and more work responsibilities. Which means I won't be at our next mediation. I have a meeting I can't miss, especially now that I have to pay for your life too!"

Melissa looks confused. "Don't you think your boss will understand it's important?"

"It's, um, too hard to explain to everyone," he says quickly.

"Oh, so no one knows? I can't keep changing our mediation because you're afraid of what others think of you!" Melissa snaps.

Fear is a primal emotional response when you perceive a threat or danger. It is normal to feel fear during and after a breakup, due to the shock of losing your relationship. Your world has been turned upside down, and your emotional stability and sense of safety have tanked. Fear can fuel anxiety, anger, or even denial about the reality of the breakup. Tom's fear that Melissa won't let him see his daughter has sent him into a tunnel of anxiety. Instead of expressing his fear directly, it comes out as anger, and he says and does things he may later regret. Fear can cloud our sense of reality, so it's hard to make good choices. Melissa is afraid of struggling financially to support herself and her daughter, a fear she has not held back on expressing to Tom.

After a breakup, with so many unknowns looming, it's normal to feel fear. You may fear losing the family house. You may fear your kids being taken away. You may fear being alone or never finding love again. You may fear the impact of the breakup on your kids. You may fear that holding to your boundaries will create conflict or a negative backlash.

Fear and anxiety are often spoken of in the same breath, but they are distinct. Unlike fear, anxiety is a generalized emotion, often without a direct object. You may be anxious about stepping into the life of single parent. You don't know how you will manage it all. Or you may be anxious about how your identity in the world will change. With all the fear and anxiety, no wonder you're not sleeping! In fact, let's look at the physical component of fear.

Fear in the Body

When you perceive that a situation is unsafe or dangerous, your brain activates what is known as the fight, flight, freeze, or fawn response. A region of the brain called the *amygdala* filters emotional information from your past memories, including any attachment wounds and traumas, to assess whether a given situation is dangerous or safe. If you sense danger, your nervous system will set off a cascade of events to protect you, even if there is no real danger. This response increases your heart rate, blood pressure, and breathing, and readies your muscles for action or inaction. You may experience chills or sweating or trembling. Your eyes and mouth may open wide. You may respond by fighting or fleeing. You may feel numb or in a daze, or even check out completely. Or you may try to appease or placate others to manage the threat.

This response happens automatically because your amygdala can overrule the prefrontal cortex, the rational part of your brain that can calmly analyze information and ask, *Am I actually in danger?* For example, as you're speaking with your co-parent, your amygdala may automatically superimpose what it recalls from your past onto what's happening in the present. Before you realize it, you've gone into a state of feeling *I need to protect myself,* even if the present situation isn't dangerous. Unless you untangle your old stuff, you may not be able to realize when your brain is confusing experiences, allowing the past to inform how you respond in the present and perpetuating fear-based reactions.

Fear in the Mind

The following are common thoughts and beliefs associated with fear after a breakup:

I'm afraid of failing.

I'm afraid of financial insecurity.

I'm afraid of rejection or abandonment.

I'm afraid I can't survive on my own.

I'm afraid of losing my kids.

I'm afraid of change.

I'm afraid of not being a good enough parent.

I'm afraid of never finding love again.

Notice if you have any of these or similar thoughts associated with fear. Become aware of how fear can manifest in your mind.

Fear and Attachment

If you are someone with secure attachment, your early caregivers were present and helped you feel protected and safe again whenever you were scared or unsure of your surroundings. As you grew up, you learned to do this for yourself. Now when you experience fear, which naturally comes with unknowns and change, you don't go into fight, flight, freeze, or fawn mode. Instead, you seek healthy ways to deal with the stresses of a breakup.

If you have avoidant attachment, you learned early on that your needs for protection and safety would not be met. You had to disconnect and retreat into your own cave to find safety. As an adult, you continue to fear you won't be safe in relationships, so you keep your distance. Your tendency to hide your feelings can make you appear rational and easy to work with as a co-parent. However, your fear of failure can make you defensive, and your preference to operate independently can make it hard to co-parent cooperatively. You may shy away from the emotionality of separation and divorce. We saw this in Tom's reluctance to tell his colleagues about his breakup, as he feared their judgment of his failed relationship.

If you have ambivalent attachment, you probably grew up feeling you couldn't rely on consistent love and reassurance from your caregivers. Their emotional state may have taken center stage, leaving you to take care of them to maintain your own sense of safety. You were constantly trying to balance their needs with yours to ensure you wouldn't be rejected. Now, your fear of being alone may be activated following a breakup, and you may try to reengage with your co-parent to alleviate it. Melissa fears losing financial security and finding herself alone. This may lead her to be overly accommodating of Tom's needs, which she later resents. As someone with ambivalent attachment, your fear of losing connection with your kids may cause you to become preoccupied with what's going on in your co-parent's home and even to project your fears of abandonment or of losing love onto your kids.

Anger

Compared with fear, anger can—though not always—be a more outwardly demonstrable emotion. It can be an expression of underlining fear and sadness.

"Why can't you answer a simple question?" Joe asks with frustration when Tanisha, his co-parent, drops off their son. Tanisha hasn't responded to his request to weigh in on a parenting decision.

"You're always coming at me with a barrage of questions," she says. "Your texts sound mad even before I've said anything! Besides, I told you I've got it handled."

Joe can feel a sudden tightness in his throat. "Well, stop ignoring me! How can I trust you when you just say you have things 'handled'? Everything's always on your terms, and I'm sick of it!" He rolls his eyes. "Maybe I'll just ignore you the next time *you* need something. Then you'll see how it feels,"

"What's the point of talking to you, Mr. Drama Queen?" Tanisha counters. "I'll see you in court!" She gets into her car, slams the door, and speeds off, tires screeching.

Anger is a normal emotion when you feel something is unjust or wrong or that your well-being or desires are threatened. It can be useful when you use it to protect and stand up for yourself. However, as a weapon against your co-parent, anger can be destructive and actually hinder you from getting what you want: to be seen and heard. Anger can be overt like Joe calling Tanisha out or indirect like Tanisha ignoring Joe's messages.

After a breakup, you can feel anger in response to not having a choice, in response to a betrayal, or in response to having been deeply hurt. Your anger can be a reaction to rejection, feelings of failure, or a sense of powerlessness. As with Tanisha and Joe, your anger may have less to do with what's happening in the moment and more to do with an accumulation of feelings ready to burst forth at the slightest excuse. You can be angry that you're alone. You can be angry about all the things you had to give up. You can be angry that your co-parent seems fine but you're not. You can be angry that your co-parent's new partner is hanging out with your child. You can be angry about broken promises or betrayals. You can be angry that your co-parent isn't following the custody plan or that you have to pay custody or spousal support.

Anger can be one step in the grief process as you try to navigate your loss. It can bring you out of numbness and give you a mouthpiece for your pain. It can feel like resentment or frustration or like wanting revenge, for example, by taking your ex to court as a way to retaliate. It can also manifest in more explosive ways, such as using threats or name-calling, as

Tanisha did, to maintain control. Following a breakup, your anger will likely be directed at your co-parent, but it can spill over into your reactions to others, including your kid, putting them in the middle of your conflict.

Anger in the Body

Anger can be verbal or nonverbal. It can be loud or silent. It can simmer internally. As you feel energy rise from your gut and move upward into your chest and head, the muscles in your stomach and chest tense up. Clenching of the jaw, glaring eyes, furrowed brows, trembling or shaking, and a flushed face are indicators of anger, as are yelling, finger pointing, aggression, and icing out.

Anger is the *fight* part of the nervous system's fight, flight, freeze, or fawn response. The amygdala senses a potential threat, and adrenaline surges, pumping through your body and getting you ready for action. When your body is in a state of anger, your prefrontal cortex is off-line, so it's hard to take in information and make rational decisions. Better to wait until you've cooled down.

Cool-down time varies from person to person. At minimum, you'll need thirty minutes before you can start to take in any information or make a rational decision. Frequent anger in the body can lead to health problems, including insomnia, stroke, high blood pressure, anxiety, and headaches.

Anger in the Mind

The following are common thoughts and beliefs associated with anger after a breakup:

I have to stand up for myself.

If I don't yell, then I won't get heard.

I have to do this on my own, and I'm pissed about it.

You hurt me. Now you'll see how it feels!

It's all your fault!

I want revenge.

I need to show I'm right.

I'm not getting what I need and deserve.

Notice if you have any of these or similar thoughts associated with anger. Become aware of how anger can manifest in your mind.

Anger and Attachment

If you are rooted in secure attachment, your early caregivers provided good models for managing anger. Now you are able to identify and validate your anger as a normal response to a painful situation that feels unjust. You can express yourself in a healthy and productive manner: you can be mindful and present, speak with confidence, and express your needs and feelings clearly and without using aggression. Even when anger arises, you remain calm and collaborate with your co-parent to work out a solution. You seek support to process your anger in a safe and healthy way.

If you have avoidant attachment, your caregivers may have given you the message that your anger, along with other emotions, was inappropriate, invalid, or an overreaction. You learned to think of anger as something you should shove down and not express, hoping it will just pass. Now, like Tanisha, you may shut down, ignore your co-parent, or leave the situation, so you can maintain a sense of control. Others may experience your withdrawal as uncaring. Or you may keep your anger on a low simmer until eventually the heat builds up so much it explodes. When Tanisha leaves, she slams the door and drives away so fast that the tires screech. You may not even realize when you're angry. You may also dismiss or admonish your child's anger, even when not directed at you, repeating the pattern of your caregivers.

If you have ambivalent attachment, you may have experienced anger as the language of your caregivers. They may have required you to get loud to make sure you were seen and validated. Now, like Joe, you may use intensity in tone to send a clear message you're angry. You may send lots of texts or overexplain yourself. Your anger may also show up as hostile, revengeful, or explosive. Angry outbursts may be turned outward toward others or inward toward yourself. You may use anger to maintain a connection with your ex. For someone with ambivalent attachment, a fight is better than silence, because being ignored feels like abandonment. You may express your anger toward your co-parent within earshot of your kid, putting them in the middle.

Shame

Whereas anger is a response to feeling wronged, shame arises when you feel that you yourself are somehow wrong or bad. This emotion is easily triggered in co-parenting conflicts, as you can see in the next scenario.

Molly clutches the phone as she talks to Carlos. "Why is it so hard to let me speak with Zia every day? When she gets home, she always cries and says she missed me."

"Zia's fine here," he counters. "You calling her at random times sucks."

"This isn't about *me*." Molly's voice is rising. "We agreed to let her call the other parent's house, and you're not letting her. You never stick to anything!"

"Well, guess what?" Carlos's voice turns icy. "Sometimes I need things on my terms."

"Geez, you're so controlling. I just want her to know I'm there for her!" Molly cries. "I don't want her to feel what I felt when my parents divorced."

"Don't worry, she knows you're there," he says. "Oh, now I get it. You want her to think you're the better parent. Ugh! This is why it's easier not to talk to you. I can't ever do anything right." Carlos hangs up before Molly can reply.

Shame is the feeling that something is fundamentally wrong or defective about who you are. You feel you're not worthy or good enough. You feel you don't live up to the expectations others have of you or you have of yourself. Shame is classified as a *self-referential* emotion, reflecting how you believe you're perceived by others. It disconnects you from others and sends you into a whirlwind of longing for worthiness and love. You can also shame others. For example, hearing Molly's criticism taps into Carlos's feeling that he's not doing a good job, so he gets defensive.

You may think—as Molly did—that shaming your co-parent will motivate them to do better. But in reality, shaming the other person will only make them feel small and powerless. Some parents use shame to teach their kids about what is bad and what is acceptable behavior. For example, shaming a child when they don't get good grades may train the child to do well in school, but the experience can also create lasting shame. When shame shows up in your adult life, it's as if the original wound were happening all over again. Shame can feel like an invisible heavy cloak you carry around that you hope no one will see.

Shame (*I am bad*) is different from guilt (*I did something bad*). While guilt allows you to take action and repair, shame leaves you feeling disempowered and shut down. You feel a need to hide parts of yourself that weren't accepted by others in your life, especially your early caregivers. When a child's needs go unmet, they tend to feel something is wrong or defective about them. It doesn't occur to them that the problem could lie with mom or dad, so it becomes *I am the problem.*

Following a breakup, shame is often the silent contender alongside other emotions. Shame is normal to feel following separation or divorce, as most of us who have been through one can attest. You're not alone! Cultural messages about divorce and single parenthood may cause shame. For example, you may feel the sting of shame when sharing the news of your breakup, as you anticipate the judgment of relatives and friends. You may feel shame in response to custody arrangements that you think imply you're a bad parent. You may feel shame if you had an affair that led to the breakup or if your ex left you for someone new. Perhaps you feel shame about failing your child or being perceived as irresponsible or not financially stable. Regardless of the trigger, your shame responds with its own internal bully voice.

Shame in the Body

Although you may want to keep shame hidden, it can be seen and felt in the body. A sunken chest and lowered head are signs of shame. You may feel smaller and even appear to shrink before others. You may feel numb, and you may avert your eyes. You may blush or sweat or even feel nauseous. Your nervous system creates these signs of the fight, flight, freeze, or fawn response, much as it would if you were in a physically dangerous situation. In the case of shame, the desire to run away or hide may arise, or you may feel paralyzed, causing you to disengage from others.

Shame in the Mind

The following are common thoughts and beliefs associated with shame after a breakup:

What if I wasn't enough?

I am not lovable.

I am unworthy.

I am a fraud.

I am defective.

I am powerless.

I am a failure.

Notice if you have any of these or similar thoughts associated with shame. Become aware of how shame can manifest in your mind.

Shame and Attachment

As a person with secure attachment, you likely had caregivers who were present and attuned. If there was a breach or a rupture of some sort while you were growing up, your caregivers made sure it was quickly repaired. They didn't leave you feeling criticized or at fault. As a result, any feelings of shame you had were short-lived. Now when someone criticizes you, you don't see yourself as fundamentally inadequate. If you do feel a moment of shame, you can be with it, without internalizing it and getting stuck or passing it on to others.

If you have avoidant attachment, you probably had caregivers who weren't present. You spent a lot of time alone and learned that to be seen as good enough, you had to be perfect. Showing your emotions didn't fit that picture of perfection. You may have thought, *I'm bad for having feelings, so I'll make them go away. Then my parents will love me.* As we saw with Carlos, perceived judgments from others can quickly evoke an *I'm unworthy* shame voice. If your co-parent triggers you, the little-kid part of you that just wants to be good enough may show up, sending you into a shame place. On the outside, you may seem calm and collected, because you want to be seen as having it all together, but internally you feel the stress of shame, causing you to isolate, disengage, or leave the situation.

If you have ambivalent attachment, your caregivers' inconsistent attention to your emotional needs made you uncertain about whether you could count on their love. Your caregivers, too preoccupied with their own needs, left you feeling unworthy. You got the message that love was conditional and based on whether you met the approval of your parents. For example, you may have thought, *When I gained weight, Mom criticized me for not being skinny like my sister. But when I got sick, she brought me soup and ice cream.* Confusing, huh? As a result, you tend to carry shame about how people perceive you and whether you are lovable and worthy. Molly's desire to be present for her child, while genuine, is fueled by the sense that she might not be seen as a worthy parent. Shame about not being enough may show up as jealousy when your co-parent finds a new partner. Or you may turn to people-pleasing behaviors, such as being overly accommodating and putting other people's needs before yours to alleviate your shame. Your longing to be loved may show up as difficulty saying no to your child or to a new partner who isn't good for your relationship with your child, or even as flirting with your ex. Shame may lead to letting other people's opinions influence you, making it hard to stick to an agreement.

Your Upstairs and Downstairs Brain

This chapter has been exploring how not only attachment styles but also the brain itself influences our experience of various emotions. Dan Siegel and Tina Payne Bryson (2012) use the metaphor of a *downstairs brain* and an *upstairs brain* to describe how this works. The downstairs brain houses the amygdala, which processes our primal emotions, such as anger, sadness, and fear. The upstairs brain, including the prefrontal cortex, is capable of more refined and complex processing. When you're dealing with all the painful stuff that comes with a breakup, you want your upstairs brain fully online. That way, you can access your capacity for higher-level processing rather than being driven by your primal emotions. This process is called *emotional regulation*. The first step is becoming aware of your emotions; the second is working with—or regulating—them. The following exercise will help you begin to do this.

Plugging Back Into Yourself

In this meditative exercise, you will tune into what you're feeling in your co-parenting relationship. Find a comfortable space and private time, and consider the following:

1. Pick a recent interaction with your co-parent and ask yourself, *How did I feel in that moment?* Recall your feeling as vividly as you can. It can be one of the four emotions we've covered or

something else. See if you can feel it as if it were happening right now. Say hello to the emotion. For example, *Hi anger, I see you.*

2. Become more curious. Where in your body do you sense this emotion? What physical sensations does it have? For example, *I feel it in my chest and throat. It feels tight.* Putting your hand on the area of the sensation can be helpful.

3. Listen to your emotion. What is it saying? What are its underlying beliefs or messages? For example, it may be telling you, *I have to be right; otherwise others will see me as a failure.*

4. Offer yourself compassion. Emotions can be scary or intimidating, but you're trying to be more vulnerable, so be kind to yourself. You might say, *It's okay. It makes sense that I feel this way,* or you might say, *This is hard.* You can also try nonverbal compassion: give yourself a hug.

5. Return to the original incident in which you felt the emotion. Has anything shifted?

6. Take a breath. You have just plugged back into yourself.

Try integrating this practice of plugging back into yourself into your daily routine. I suggest doing it as a meditative exercise after your encounters with your co-parent. As you become more experienced, you'll feel comfortable doing it in the heat of moment as well.

In this chapter, we have looked closely at the most common emotions co-parents grapple with. Recognizing these emotions and beginning to understand and make sense of your own emotional stuff is the first step setting you up to work more effectively with your co-parent. In the next chapter, we'll cover the second step: learning to respond rather than react when you come up against your co-parent's stuff. But before moving on, let's look at some more questions that I hear frequently from co-parents.

● ● Now What? ● ●

Question: "Do I have to break my attachment to my co-parent before I can untangle my emotional cables?"

Answer: Untangling your emotional cables is part of the process of breaking the attachment. As you begin to notice when and how you reach out to your co-parent to meet your emotional needs—and practice plugging back into yourself instead—your attachment will decrease. The "Plugging Back Into Yourself" exercise will help you do this. It will give you the validation you need to prepare yourself to step into the arena of co-parenting.

Question: "My kids pick up on my sadness. Seems like it makes them sad too. How do I protect them?"

Answer: Your kids will have their own sadness. These are beautiful moments to talk about emotions. You might say, "I feel sad, but I'm okay. It's normal to feel sad when things change. How do you feel about all the changes? Are you sometimes sad?" You can't protect your kids from their emotions, but you can make sure they don't feel responsible for taking care of yours. Being mindful of your child's feelings will allow them to separate their feelings from yours.

Question: "Is it possible to feel afraid and angry at the same time?"

Answer: Absolutely. Anger is one way we express fear. Fear is a more vulnerable emotion than anger because it taps into our core sense of safety. Feeling anger can be a signal you're actually afraid. You may be using anger to protect the part of you that's afraid. Use the "Plugging Back Into Yourself" exercise to explore how fear and anger show up for you.

Question: "My co-parent keeps pointing out things I'm not doing right. I end up feeling like a bad parent. How do I stop that?"

Answer: It sounds like your co-parent may be triggering feelings of shame you learned early in life, especially as those feelings relate to other people's expectations. You can start by being curious about your own stuff. Your co-parent doesn't have to change for your feelings to change. First notice the *shoulds* and other negative beliefs you place on yourself. Listen to the ways your internal bully speaks to you. Notice how unkind it is. Is what it says even true? Next, try saying the belief aloud, as if to a child or a friend. How does that feel? Does it help? What can you say to yourself that would be kinder and truer?

Chapter 3

Responding Instead of Reacting

Remember that game of hot potato you played at childhood parties? No one wanted the potato, so the goal was to pass it on as fast as you could. I like to think of sadness, fear, anger, and shame as hot-potato emotions. We try to pass them on to someone else—in this case, our co-parent. This is understandable. Sitting with pain and vulnerabilities is uncomfortable, and it seems easier to react in ways that protect you from feeling and acknowledging what's going on for you inside. You've probably also noticed your co-parent trying to pass their stuff on to you. Maybe you've thought, *I have enough of my own, thanks!* But the game goes on, each of you still looking to the other to carry the load. This game is no fun and usually ends up hurting the kids more than anyone.

Your behavioral reactions to your co-parent grow out of the various emotions we discussed in chapter 2. A *behavioral reaction* is based on thoughts and feelings. In and of itself, it's neither positive nor negative. For example, you see your child. You feel all warm and fuzzy and think, *I love you!* Based on that, your positive reaction is to hug your child. Or to take a negative example, you see your co-parent with a new partner and have the fear-based thought *They're going to replace me.* It doesn't matter what's really going to happen; your thoughts and emotions are enough to trigger you to lash out reactively and say something nasty to your co-parent.

It is hard to make rational decisions and have calm interactions when you're emotionally triggered. It is easier to just react in the moment. In fact, what you want to do is *respond*. You want to use the executive functions of your brain, centered in the prefrontal cortex, rather than give your reactive amygdala full reign. Switching from reaction to response isn't easy, but you can learn to do this by becoming more mindful, through pausing, observing, and choosing to shift your reactive impulses.

In this chapter, we're going to examine the most common behavioral reactions after a breakup. All of them involve control, in one way or another. We will start by looking at general control-seeking behaviors, including passive and active forms of aggression. Then we'll discuss blame and criticism. You may identify with some of these reactions more than others, or you may identify with all of them. You may also recognize the reactions of your co-parent, which can give you valuable insights into their interactions with you. Keep in mind, however, that in this chapter, you are still focusing on *your* stuff. The purpose here is first to understand how your attachment behaviors show up—what you tend to say and do to protect yourself from feeling fear, anger, and shame—and second to discover alternative responses that are not reactive. If you and your co-parent can stop playing hot potato with your emotions, you can finally untangle the emotional cables still keeping you bound to each other.

Control-Seeking Behaviors

Have you noticed how much energy you put into trying to figure out what your co-parent is doing and why? That effort may take the form of reactive, control-seeking behavior. You may try to control them because you're feeling unsafe and afraid of more loss, or as a means of getting or doing things your way. Your inner bully might be screaming that you're powerless or that your needs aren't being recognized. Or control may be your way of proving yourself or seeking revenge. All these insecurities and the emotions of sadness, fear, anger, and shame may be swirling within you, but you don't know how to or don't want to acknowledge them—especially not to your co-parent! Instead, your knee-jerk reaction is to try to manage your co-parent and focus on *their* wrongdoings, so you can feel safe, in control, or right. Common controlling behaviors include the following:

- Shutting down communication, stonewalling (icing out, ignoring)

- Cutting off financial access and resources

- Withholding information or access (not allowing the co-parent to see or talk to the kids)

- Micromanaging what's going on in the co-parent's home

- Being inflexible on scheduling requests

- Being defensive, always needing to be right

- Using the child to hurt the co-parent (such as making false or negative comments)

- Overaccommodating

- Manipulating

Let's see how this plays out with co-parents Cammy and Blake. First we'll look at the ways they seek to control each other. Then we'll see what happens when one of them chooses to respond rather than react.

• Cammy and Blake: Take 1

"Jamie is always tired when I get him. I thought we decided on one hour of video games after homework. But it's as if we never had that conversation. You know too much video time is bad for his sleep," Blake says into the phone.

"You decided that, not me," Cammy snaps back. "You don't even know whether he played any video games here last week. Besides, I'm sick of you telling me what to do. It was like this when we were

*together. You always thought you knew better." She can feel tension
building in her chest.*

*"That's not true!" Blake's voice rises as he starts to speak faster.
"Every time I try to talk, you cut me off or don't respond. I've been
trying to reach you for days now."*

"I'm busy," Cammy says, her voice strained.

*"That's no excuse. We agreed you would always respond within
twenty-four hours. Cam, I just want you to be honest with me!"*

*"Oh, so you're calling me a liar? I don't need this." Cammy hangs
up the phone.*

*Blake continues over text. "We lost connection. I want to settle
this about video time and talk about vacation. I don't want you taking
him to New York."*

No response.

*He sends another text a few minutes later. "Answer me!" In his
mind, he's thinking,* No way am I letting her take him to New York
during my time.

No response.

Cammy and Blake are engaged in a typical co-parenting defensive
battle over who knows best. The need to control in such situations may be
cloaked in "doing what's best for the child," but it's really more about each
of them trying to quell their own fears or shame.

With ambivalent tendencies, Blake talks a lot. It's one of his ways of
maintaining a sense of control. He is upset because Cammy has not been
responsive, which angers him and triggers his fear of rejection. With avoidant tendencies, Cammy uses being unresponsive as a silent but powerful
tool to control her environment. Here, Blake hands the hot potato of his
anger and fear of rejection to Cammy through his accusations and desire
to be overly involved in her household. She picks it up, and the heat of his
fear triggers her own shame about not doing things right. So she throws
the potato right back at him. Holding the steaming potato sends him into
a place of not feeling valued, so he escalates his accusations in an attempt
to prove himself and regain control. This sends Cammy into a state of

overwhelm, so she hangs up, which is the only way she knows to control the situation. Feeling the rejection from being hung up on, Blake is angry to the point of grasping at ways to punish Cammy—the only way he feels he has some power.

Both co-parents have a role in this interaction. One's behavioral reaction sets off the other's, and off they go into their familiar conflict. As you read take 2, see what Cammy does differently to reduce her own control-seeking behavior and how this influences Blake's response.

• Cammy and Blake: Take 2

"Jamie is always tired when I get him. I thought we decided on one hour of video games after homework. But it's as if we never had that conversation. You know too much video time is bad for his sleep," Blake says into the phone.

Cammy feels herself becoming triggered, so she pauses and takes a breath to calm herself before responding. "I hear your concern about Jamie being tired. I agree about making sure he gets enough sleep. We're working out his video time, and I hope you can trust me to have it under control."

"Okay…but I've been trying to reach you for days." Blake's voice rises as he starts to speak faster.

Cammy recognizes that her ignoring Blake triggers him. She also understands that ignoring his calls is her cover for being seen as doing things wrong. Instead of getting defensive, she takes a breath and acknowledges her vulnerability. "I know I need to respond sooner. I'm working on that."

"Thanks for saying that," Blake says, feeling an unexpected flash of relief. "Do you remember us agreeing to respond within twenty-four hours?"

"Yeah, but it would help if we could set specific times to talk. Then I can plan ahead rather than trying to do things at the last minute," Cammy says.

"That's fine. We need to talk about Jamie's video games," Blake says. "And there are other issues too. Like vacation travel."

Cammy feels her overwhelm start to creep in but resists the temptation to give Blake the brush-off. "Can we talk tomorrow at six o'clock? I don't have time right now."

"How about seven?" Blake suggests. "That'd be better for me."

"Sounds good." Cammy lets out a breath as she puts down her phone.

Notice that even though only one of the co-parents changed their tone and reactions, they both moved toward greater cooperation, and the outcome of their interaction changed dramatically. This may not always work out smoothly on the first try, but taking care of your own stuff and minimizing your own controlling behaviors is the most effective way to untangle the cables that still plug you into your ex. Instead of handing your co-parent the hot potato of your emotions, see if you can set it aside and get on with business.

Now that you've seen control-seeking behaviors in action, let's look at the active and passive forms these behaviors can take.

Active and Passive Aggression

Control-seeking behaviors can be expressions of aggression toward a co-parent. *Active aggression* includes yelling, rage, threatening, and using a hostile or condescending tone (verbally or through emails or text). Your co-parent most likely will take your behavior as an attack and become defensive instead of listening to your need, request, or boundary statement. *Passive aggression* includes ignoring or only giving partial info to your co-parent, making excuses, procrastinating, being defensive, not following through on agreements, overaccommodating, people pleasing, and weaponized kindness.

Yelling may feel good, as if you're finally standing up for yourself, but it can be both addictive and contagious. In the moment, you may feel a surge of energy rise through your core and out your mouth. However, once you get started, and your nervous system is fired up, this kind of reaction is hard to stop. Plus, your co-parent may feel entitled to get in on the act. In fact, what's probably happening is you're acting out the powerlessness you felt as a kid, using yelling to be heard and to gain a sense of control. This serves to push people away, even though what you really want is to be seen and understood.

When you threaten your co-parent, you're really saying, "I'm scared and feel powerless and small, but I don't want you to see that, so instead I'll threaten you. That way, I can feel big and make you feel small." You're passing your hot potato of fear and shame to your co-parent in the form of a threat. Or vice versa. Threats can be active ("If you do that, I won't let you see the kids") or passive ("If I were you, I wouldn't keep pushing that custody discussion").

Passive aggression avoids overt conflict but is still loaded with subtle negativity. You may use passive aggression if you grew up in an environment where expressing anger or upset got you in trouble. Now you do it with your co-parent to punish them while still maintaining an appearance of niceness. Although you may think being overly accommodating is effective, this is rarely the case. For example, you may agree to your co-parent's fifth request for a schedule change, hoping they'll do the same for you when you need it...only to find out that they won't. Or you don't hold boundaries with your child when they're upset about not getting what they want at the other parent's home...only to have your child develop behavior problems at school. In each instance, you feel like you're managing the situation and taking control, but you aren't creating the safety, security, or validation you really seek. Neither your needs nor your co-parent's needs are met. And your child stands to suffer the most.

Blaming Behaviors

Blaming is a control-seeking behavior that focuses on fault finding. It's a defensive strategy to protect your sense of self in response to a mistake or something difficult that happened between you and your co-parent. It's a way of avoiding accountability. As a child, being wrong may have meant you were bad, or you may have felt blamed for no good reason; therefore, as an adult, you react by blaming others. The instinct to blame usually comes from feeling inadequate or not wanting to feel emotionally unsafe. Blaming your co-parent is a way of passing that hot potato of shame on to them, sending them into a shame spiral.

In the moment, blaming your co-parent may feel like it puts you in control. However, because your goal is to work with your co-parent as an effective team, lording control over them will only backfire. Some common blame behaviors are dodging responsibility by flipping the story ("It happened because *you* were late. What else was I supposed to do?" or "You're the one who…") and making accusations ("You always ignore her," "You never help with his homework," or "You always forget"). Related defensive behaviors, such as denial ("I never said that" or "I don't remember") and minimizing ("So what? It doesn't matter"), can land much like blaming.

Let's see how co-parents Jade and Kwan use blame behaviors to try to control each other.

• Jade and Kwan: Take 1

Jade sends out a text at 10:30 p.m. "You always let Sheena get away with not doing her homework. Now her grades are falling behind."

"WTF?" Kwan responds, annoyed. "She does her homework here. If she got a poor grade, it's because you're always too busy to help her."

"Have you forgotten I own a small business?" Jade shoots back. "This grade problem is all on you!"

"It's always about your work. You're not there for Sheena, just like you were never there for me when I needed you." Kwan feels himself getting tense.

"So now you're telling her lies about me? Lately she's complained about being here. I think it's because you coddle her so much," Jade responds.

"Just telling the truth as I see it," Kwan texts back. A slight smile forms on his face as he rereads the text. Despite a tinge of guilt, he's proud Sheena prefers to be with him.

Jade and Kwan's hot potato blame game most likely didn't start with the demise of their relationship. They are clearly adept at faulting each other, so neither has to look like the bad guy or take ownership of their part in the dynamic. Their exchange quickly becomes all about the two of them and their needs, not about Sheena's grades.

Jade blames Kwan for any issues with their daughter, because that way she doesn't have to get in touch with her fears about not being successful enough and independent, which are triggered in this conversation. Kwan gets defensive and deflects the blame back to Jade, so he can avoid feeling he isn't a good enough parent. This triggers Jade's own not-doing-it-right button. So she doesn't have to feel angry about being alone, she hurls back the accusations, adding more fuel to Kwan's shame about being seen as capable. The sting of this shame leads him to blame her for not being there for him, as he returns the now fully loaded potato in the blame game.

At the end, Kwan sits back, having taken no responsibility and having done nothing to break the cycle of blame between Jade and him. He gets some satisfaction from feeling he won because their daughter prefers to be with him. Winning for him means he has proven himself to be without fault.

Let's see what Kwan can do to shift his reactive behavior and how this shift affects the outcome of the interaction between Jade and him. Their take 2 takes place after Kwan has worked with the "Plugging Back Into Yourself" exercise (in chapter 2) and begun to get more in touch with his emotions.

• Jade and Kwan: Take 2

Jade sends out a text at 10:30 p.m. "You always let Sheena get away with not doing her homework. Now her grades are falling behind."

Feeling triggered by the message, Kwan pauses before responding. Checking his body, he notices tension in his shoulder muscles. It's a familiar feeling he gets whenever Jade blames him for something he feels isn't his fault. He also remembers the underlying message of this feeling: Leave me alone. I can deal with this on my own! Then he remembers that things get worse if he ignores Jade, so he texts back, "We should talk about her grades. How about tomorrow?"

"I'll be on my own at the shop. I won't have time," Jade responds, still feeling resentful. She's about to send another text, blaming Kwan for gatekeeping when they can talk, but stops herself and risks a direct question that reflects her needs: "How about right now?"

Kwan recognizes that Jade is upset, but he also wants to make sure this doesn't become an all-night affair. "Okay. Just a few minutes. So, what do you think is going on with Sheena?"

Jade notices that her breath has slowed down and she feels a little less panicky. Kwan is listening. "Actually, it's not just the grades. Lately she seems unhappy when she's here. Have you said anything negative about me to her?"

"Well, you are super busy. That's not news." He adds a winking face emoji to his text, so Jade won't feel blamed. "But no, I haven't. Sheena does mention you're busy a lot. I didn't know she was unhappy, though."

Jade laughs knowingly to herself. Even though Kwan resented her work during their relationship, he was always proud of her drive. "All right, I'll make time tomorrow at noon. I'd like to talk more about these two things," she texts back.

This interaction stays more focused on the child. Each co-parent is able to make requests and express concerns from their own perspective, instead of engaging in knee-jerk blaming behavior. They are also setting themselves up for an in-person meeting, where they can move toward secure attachment, be more collaborative, and find solutions to what might be going on with their daughter.

Criticizing Behaviors

Criticism is a judgment that focuses on who is right or wrong or on what is bad about your co-parent. It devalues your co-parent and sends the message that you know better or don't trust them. Expressing criticism is a means of controlling the outside world, so you can feel safer in your inside world. It displaces the discomfort that comes up in a situation when you don't like or don't understand something. It can cover a need or displace shame that you're not good enough. Focusing on what the other person is doing is a way to manage your own anxiety or stress. "You're not doing it right" is code for "I'm scared" or "I'm inadequate," which means "I'm unlovable."

If you were criticized by a caregiver growing up, you may automatically resort to criticism as a way to thrust your hot potato of fear or shame toward your co-parent. If you're holding on to a lot of unspoken complaints and built-up resentments, you may think criticizing your co-parent or child will get them to change. You may think it will keep you or your child safer. However, criticism doesn't actually get your need met or allow you to communicate with your co-parent or help you determine whether your child is actually safe. Unless you have a clear reason to believe your child is not safe with their other parent, criticism will only lead to a defensive reaction and not to solutions for better caring for your child.

Couples therapist John Gottman calls criticism the first of the "four horsemen" that are destructive for any relationship (Lisitsa 2013). The other three (stonewalling, contempt, and defensiveness) are control-seeking behaviors. Criticism often goes hand in hand with blame; you simultaneously point out your co-parent's flaws and assign fault. Some common criticizing behaviors are attacking the other's character ("You're lazy"), making judgments ("You're not doing it right"), making comparisons ("My new partner understands me better than you ever could"), and name-calling ("You're a deadbeat parent").

Let's see how co-parents Penelope and Lisa use some of these criticizing behaviors with each other.

- *Penelope and Lisa: Take 1*

   "I know you don't think being clean is important, but every time I pick up the boys, they're always in their filthy old T-shirts," Penelope says to her co-parent over the phone. She's angry because she didn't plan

enough time when picking up the twins and arrived late for their three-year wellness checkup at the doctor's. "What happened to those new T-shirts I bought them?"

"I'm doing the best I can," Lisa responds. "But usually they've just come in from playing outside. No time to change them."

"Your best isn't cutting it, obviously. They aren't learning good hygiene from you," Penelope says. "Maybe do laundry sometimes! I'm sick of buying clothes I never see!"

"You have no idea how often I ask them to change their clothes and wash their hands. Even at their age, they have their favorite shirts. I'm not going to do battle over everything. Geez, can't you ever relax?" Lisa says. "Stop being so OCD," she adds under her breath.

"Huh? Did you just call me OCD?"

Lisa doubles down on her accusation. "What I'm saying is other parents don't seem to care as much as you. They're not neat freaks, like you."

"Well, you don't have kids with those parents," Penelope snaps back. "And it's not OCD. I guess now that you're getting a psychology degree, you think you can analyze me. Do you even know what OCD means?"

"Whatever." Lisa rolls her eyes as she puts her phone down.

Penelope and Lisa are engaged in a common co-parenting critical-defensive cycle. Penelope uses the issue of cleanliness to feel in control. Instead of directly expressing what she needs, she balls up her fears about not being a perfect co-parent and stuffs them into the hot potato she hands off to Lisa.

Lisa picks it up and is immediately defensive because it taps into her own desire not to disappoint others. She takes the expectations Penelope has handed her, mixes in her own feelings of inadequacy as a parent and resentment toward Penelope, tosses in a bit of name-calling, and throws the potato back. This triggers Penelope's need to defend her own sense of self. She stands her ground and fires back full force, trying to assert her position of "I know better than you."

Both co-parents are seeking safety and fear being out of control. Acknowledging they could do better would feel too vulnerable and risky. Instead, they hide behind their own internalized critic and rely on criticism and defensive behaviors to maintain a facade of control.

Let's see what happens when Lisa, instead of getting defensive, uses the "Plugging Back Into Yourself" exercise to reconnect, ground, and understand what her real needs are.

• *Penelope and Lisa: Take 2*

"I know you don't think being clean is important, but every time I pick up the boys, they're always in their filthy old T-shirts," Penelope says to her co-parent over the phone. "What happened to those new T-shirts I bought them?"

Lisa can feel her stomach tighten and a wave of pain surge through her. She feels shame at being called unclean and wants to defend herself. But she takes a moment, breathes in deeply, and acknowledges how her shame reflects her ambivalent attachment and taps into her old childhood stuff about feeling unworthy of love. She also knows that reacting to this criticism won't help. So she puts a smile on her face and makes an effort to focus instead on the facts, the kids, and what she knows to be true. "They definitely get dirty!" she responds lightly. "Want me to pack those T-shirts in their bags next time?"

"Yeah, thanks," Penelope says, surprised she isn't facing any pushback. Then she adds, "But it's not only about the shirts. It's not too soon to start teaching them good hygiene habits."

Again, Lisa lets the implied criticism roll off her and responds without getting defensive. "I agree, hygiene is important. Let's get on the same page about what to focus on that's also age appropriate. Today doesn't work for me. How about this weekend?"

"Okay, it's a deal," Penelope says.

Lisa has spent time discovering the body cues that let her know she is triggered and recognizing how her attachment style kicks in. Instead of taking the critical bait, she sets it aside and agrees it's important for the kids to learn about hygiene. Because Lisa can see that Penelope's combative style is not her own stuff and doesn't reflect on her, she can avoid her own criticizing behavior without feeling she is losing anything.

Stop Playing Hot Potato with Your Emotions

Now that you are more aware of your feelings and have explored some of the main behavioral reactions co-parents have to such feelings, you can quit playing the hot potato game with your emotions and begin to respond rather than simply react in a triggering situation. The following process may sound like a lot to do in the midst of an interaction—and initially you may need to go through these steps *after* interacting with your co-parent—but as you become more familiar with the process, it will become second nature and you can do it in real time. Here are the steps.

Pause and Identify Your Emotion

When you feel triggered to react, pause and name the emotion. Observe any sensations and where you feel them in your body. See if you can also identify what triggered the emotion. This may be obvious (*My co-parent didn't return my call, so I'm angry*) or more subtle (*Being alone over the holiday, I felt sad and ashamed because it seems like no one cares about me*). You may feel one emotion or multiple emotions; see if you can distinguish them. As you notice each emotion, identify the thoughts and beliefs associated with it.

Observe and Identify Your Reaction

As we've seen, behavioral reactions often occur very quickly due to the instinct to protect yourself. You don't want to feel the heat of the emotional potato, so you pass it before it fully lands in your body. As a result, you may not be aware of your reaction. The point here is to slow down and observe what you have an urge to do. Shut down? Get defensive or try to prove yourself? Blame or criticize your co-parent? Send lots of aggressive texts or emails? Go into people-pleasing mode?

Ask If This Is Helpful

Knowing both your emotions and your behavioral reactions allows you to begin to shift the pattern. One of the most effective techniques is to ask yourself, *Will my behavior help me get my needs met or my requests heard? Will it allow me to make good decisions for myself and for our child? Is what I'm doing helping or hurting?* When you ask this, be fully honest with yourself. Remember, this is just you talking with yourself, dealing with your own stuff. Most likely, as you start to ask these questions, you will realize that many of your behavioral reactions aren't helpful.

Ask What Would Be More Helpful

Finally, for each behavioral reaction you determine is not helpful, you'll want to have some alternative responses in your repertoire. This way, you can stop playing hot potato with your emotions. Here are several strategies you can bring to interactions with your co-parent. All are designed to shift you out of a reactive mode and into a more secure, calmer, and more mindful response. We will revisit many of these strategies in greater detail in the following chapters.

- Stop and take a break. This could include thinking about your personal peaceful place, taking a few breaths, noticing sensations in your body, exercising, taking a bath, cuddling with your pet, calling a friend, drawing, or journaling. (Note that a break is an intentional pause, not an excuse to ignore or ghost your co-parent.)

- Examine the facts of the situation. What is actually true? For example, are you or is your child actually in danger? Are you actually out of control? What was your agreement? Before you respond to your co-parent, weigh what is important for you, what you need, and what you can set aside.

- Distinguish between your stuff and your co-parent's stuff. Remember that you're only responsible for your own stuff.

- When responding to your co-parent, keep the focus of discussion on your kid. Focus on one topic at a time and don't let the conversation become personal.

Ultimately, you want to be able to recognize your go-to behavioral reaction in a particular situation before you react. To bring this awareness with you going forward, I suggest doing the following exercise.

Converting Reactions into Responses

Find a quiet time to sit with yourself and reflect on the following questions. Be honest and kind. We all go into self-protective states when our stuff gets triggered, so you're not alone.

1. What interactions with your co-parent are emotional triggers for you? Make a list.

2. In each interaction, do you react by general control-seeking? Blaming? Criticizing?

3. Can you see any patterns? Here are some examples: ignoring or not responding when your co-parent makes requests you don't like, being overly accommodating to keep the peace, criticizing your co-parent when they do something you don't like, and getting defensive so you can always seem right.

4. Finally, for each of your triggering interactions, identify alternative responses that would be more helpful.

Developing greater awareness will help you feel empowered so you can choose responsive rather than reactive ways to communicate with your co-parent, which will lead to better outcomes.

Congratulations on your hard work! We're about to dive into the six principles of successful co-parenting, beginning with the principle of commitment. Before moving on, here are a few questions I frequently hear.

● ● **Now What?** ● ●

Question: "Will knowing my and my co-parent's attachment styles help me be less reactive?"

Answer: Absolutely! Understanding your attachment styles can make it easier to recognize both your emotional triggers. For example, if your co-parent gets reactive whenever you offer a suggestion, it could be because their avoidant tendencies make them sensitive to criticism. Knowing this, you can check in with yourself: *Am I using a tone that could come off as critical?* Even if the answer is no, you can reframe your comment, so it doesn't insinuate that your co-parent did something wrong. Or you can simply set it aside, because that is who they are and you can't change it.

Question: "How can it help if only I change *my* behavior? Won't I just become a victim?"

Answer: Conflict occurs between two people. If you respond in a way that is free of your stuff, then you aren't handing your co-parent a hot potato. Or if you refuse to catch the hot potato they're tossing at you, you won't take on their stuff. By not engaging in the hot potato game, that game stops. You may not be able to stop your co-parent's behavior, but you can stop your own response. Then, instead of being a victim, you'll feel empowered, knowing you can make choices and respond in ways that work better for *you*.

Question: "Can control-seeking behavior ever be a good response, or is it always just reactive?"

Answer: It depends on what your intention is behind the behavior. For example, suppose you have to remind your co-parent about soccer practice, or otherwise he'll forget. Is this micromanaging? It could be, if you're doing it to prove you're the better parent or to criticize your co-parent. But if this is about your child having both their parents present, it would count as teamwork rather than control-seeking behavior.

Chapter 4

Creating Certainty Amid Change

Being romantic partners and being co-parents are two separate and distinct relationships, but you can have them with the same person at different times. I like to visualize the transition between these as the flipping of a triangle that represents your family. As mathematicians and architects tell us, a triangle is the strongest shape. When the two of you were romantic partners, a horizontal line formed between you; this connection became the top side of an equilateral triangle after your child came into your union. Your child was at the bottom point. All the parenting and nurturing operating in one household flowed down the sides of the triangle to your child. Now that you've separated, your romantic relationship has ended, but your parenting relationship has not, so this triangle needs to flip (see figure 1). It's still a strong shape, but the focus has shifted away from your adult relationship and toward your kid. Your kid moves to the top of the triangle, and you two parents become the supporting base, working together in two households to achieve a win-win. As your team effort flows up to your kid, and you commit to prioritizing their needs, a win-win-win becomes possible.

Kid

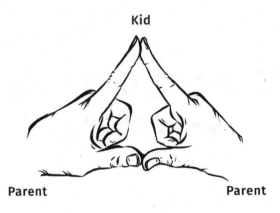

Parent   **Parent**

Figure 1: The Co-Parenting Triangle

Each side of your co-parenting triangle may grow or bend at its own rate as you and your co-parent develop your respective attachments with your kid. Despite its flexibility—and sometimes even because of it—the flipped triangle provides the most stable system for your kid to feel safe and secure. In fact, research tells us that the quality of co-parenting a child or adolescent receives, including the co-parents' ability to cooperate and provide a united front, is the key element predicting the child's mental health, self-esteem, and academic achievement after a separation or divorce (Lamela and Figueiredo 2016).

The six principles of engagement for successful co-parenting will help you shore up and fortify the sides of your triangle by creating both a co-parenting relationship and a parenting relationship (with your kid) that are grounded in secure attachment. These principles will help you define your cooperative co-parenting relationship, so you and your co-parent can prioritize what's best for your kid, thereby greatly reducing the negative impact of your breakup. Cooperative co-parenting creates secure kids.

Committing to Being a Co-parenting Team

This chapter introduces the principle of *commitment*: co-parents create certainty in the midst of change by committing to show up and be present for their child, thereby creating trust and reducing anxiety. We'll look at what commitment means within a co-parenting relationship. Then we'll examine the main steps to establishing commitment: making a clean break, making a foundational agreement, and tending to your commitment so it remains vital.

You and your co-parent don't ever have to become best friends for the principles of engagement to be effective. You can keep working through your own feelings about the dissolution of the relationship, as you move toward forming a co-parenting team that operates in a cordial or business-like fashion to prioritize the needs of your child. Think of it like a non-profit whose sole purpose is to raise a healthy and secure kid. This will have head-in-your-hands frustration moments, but it will also have elated, empowering moments. So buckle up for the ride; in the end, it will be worth it!

• *Gabriel and Kate*

"Our teacher conference is this afternoon," Gabriel tells his co-parent after dropping off their daughter at school. "I'm calling to remind you because you skipped the last one." He frowns to himself, thinking, And the one before that too.

"Yeah, Lilly mentioned yesterday that you told her to remind me," Kate says distractedly, juggling her phone and her new baby as she prepares to bathe him. Time for a school meeting doesn't factor in.

Gabriel can sense he's not making it onto Kate's radar, so he pushes harder. "The teacher is expecting both of us. He wants to know why Lilly's grades have fallen this semester."

That stops Kate in her tracks. "What's going on with her grades?"

"Geez! We both get the same emails from her teacher!" Gabriel waits for Kate to acknowledge that. When she doesn't, he fills in the blanks. "She's close to failing math, and she's struggling in social studies."

"Right, right," Kate says quickly, hoping Gabriel won't realize she hasn't read the teacher's recent emails. "She's always welcome to ask

for help with her homework when she's here. What I don't need is you breathing down my neck. You know I'm busy with the baby. My house, my rules, remember."

"Um, no," Gabriel says. "This is about Lilly. You need to be more involved in her education. Of course, your baby is important, but since his birth, Lilly hasn't been doing well at school. What do I have to say to get you to come to the teacher conference today?"

"All right, I'll try," Kate says. "That means bringing the baby, though."

What's wrong with this scenario? For starters, Kate is disengaged from her daughter's education. She isn't paying attention to what's happening at school and isn't taking an active role in helping Lilly with her homework. It's understandable a new baby would cause some changes, but that shouldn't keep Kate from teaming up with Gabriel to support their daughter. In his attempt to get Kate to show up for the teacher conference, Gabriel puts Lilly in the middle as the messenger. And when he tries to reason with Kate, he resorts to blaming her. Neither co-parent has made the commitment to parent together. As a result, both are stressed out. And Lilly is the one who stands to lose the most. She isn't getting the security and support she needs, and the outcome of that is reflected in her performance at school.

What Commitment Means

A commitment is an intentional choice. Committing to a person means having the dedication to follow through on actions even if it's challenging at times; it's about putting all your chips in with that person. When you and the person who is now your ex entered a committed romantic relationship, you made promises to each other. Now, without the certitude provided by those promises, your relationship lacks security and trust. No one knows what to expect or whom they can count on. Transitioning from one home to two homes can create many unknowns and anxieties for your child and disrupt their attachment system. The best way to ease this uncertainty is for you and your co-parent to commit now to functioning as a secure and cooperative co-parenting team.

You may be reluctant to consider any form of commitment to your ex. After all, didn't you just end that committed relationship? Didn't you discover you can't count on your ex? They didn't show up as a parent while you were together, so why would they start now? Or maybe you are feeling so betrayed or hurt that the idea of committing seems out of the question. With so many unknowns, the idea of commitment can feel scary or confusing. These are legitimate concerns. But hear me out. I'm not asking you to revive old vows. Rather, this is an invitation to create a new co-parenting commitment that is really a commitment to your child.

Consider the Benefits

Being in a secure, committed co-parenting relationship offers some powerful benefits. When you co-parent as a team, both of you increase your resources of time, money, and support. You also give yourselves a mechanism to minimize threats and anxiety. This in turn allows both of you more space for your individual emotional growth and well-being. You have more energy for your own creativity and interests and can be more productive at work. You increase your chances of developing new healthy romantic relationships. You can also develop a stronger relationship with your child.

Parenting on your own can be stressful. Committing to being a co-parenting team reduces that stress. The two of you may even find you work better together as co-parents than you did as romantic partners. Your co-parent may step up and be more present as a parent, because now the focus of your relationship is only on parenting.

Your child will benefit from having committed co-parents. This commitment is an act of love for your child. What children fear most following a separation or divorce is losing a parent. Seeing your commitment to co-parenting helps your child be certain this won't happen. This certainty provides a sense of safety and gives your child the freedom to continue to form secure attachments with both parents. Your commitment grants your child the space to think, *What a relief! Thanks, parents. Now can I get back to hanging out with my friends, making things, and growing out of my clothes!*

Committed Co-Parenting and Attachment Styles

Psychologist Gordon Neufeld and physician Gabor Maté (2014) talk about the importance of parents being their child's compass point to provide the guidance, direction, and boundaries their kid needs. This is a good metaphor for providing secure attachment. When you break up, your child still needs both of you to help navigate the murky waters of separation. Your attachment style, however, may affect your readiness to commit to co-parenting.

If you have secure attachment, you can enter into a co-parenting commitment with ease. You respect boundaries and follow through with agreements. You stay open and listen to the other parent's perspective. You also allow space for your co-parent to be more present as a parent, thus increasing certainty for you, your co-parent, and your kid.

If you have avoidant attachment, commitment can feel stifling, and the risk of being let down may keep you from even thinking about committing. You may also see it as restricting your independence. You may want to avoid a co-parenting commitment or find excuses about why it would be silly or unnecessary. In the earlier example, Kate, who has avoidant attachment, finds ways—without even realizing it—to dodge committing to her responsibilities as a co-parent. Alternatively, you may be rigid and inflexible when you do commit.

If you have ambivalent attachment, you may use commitment to stay too close to your co-parent, reengage emotionally, or become overinvolved in your co-parent's life. Gabriel's ambivalent attachment leads him to remain entangled with Kate even though she's moved on with a new partner. You may also use commitment to promote your own emotional needs; alternatively, you may be overly accommodating with your co-parent.

This is all to say that some co-parents will be more open to teamwork than others are. For this process to succeed, however, your co-parent must be at least minimally involved.

Three Steps to Commitment

Here are three steps you can take with your co-parent to form an effective team.

1. Make a clean break.

2. Make a foundational agreement.

3. Tend to your commitment.

As I go into each of these steps, I will suggest how to work with it, depending on the openness of your co-parent.

Make a Clean Break

This initial step is intended to clear the air, so you and your co-parent can leave your romantic relationship in the rearview mirror and make the intentional choice to be a co-parenting team. I also suggest setting aside time to informally address any emotional entanglements left over from your romantic relationship. Doing this will help you to separate the parenting aspects from the romantic aspects of your relationship and to refocus your commitment on working together as a team, for the sake of your child. You can view it as an intentional reframing of your relationship, to flip the triangle so your child is at the top.

Let's consider Kate and Gabriel's need for a clean break before they can commit to co-parenting together. Kate was already in a close friendship with a new partner before she and Gabriel split up. Although Gabriel isn't trying to get back at her, he remains emotionally entangled. Even three years later, anger, hurt, and pain bubble up for him in the form of criticism and underhanded comments when they interact as co-parents. He can't forget that she was never fully present for him in the ways he wanted. For her part, Kate harbors anger at her ex because she feels he was calling all the shots when they were together. She continues to push him away—and sometimes their daughter as well—to maintain her sense of control and independence. Without a clean break, these co-parents will continue to reactivate their old wounds. Both their daughter and Kate's new baby will be caught in the crossfire.

It may be tempting to think that either you or your co-parent, or both of you, are beyond the need for a clean break. And that's possible. Nevertheless, even if you and your ex mutually agreed to end your relationship, two individuals rarely process loss and heal at the same rate. You most likely will continue to have emotional responses to each other and to changes in your situation. You may find yourself thinking, *I'm fine; they're the ones with the issue* or *I wish they'd get over it*. Or you may feel, *They've obviously moved on, so why can't I get there?* In my experience, regardless of where new co-parents fall on the healing spectrum, the vast majority can benefit from intentionally and explicitly agreeing to make a clean break.

I suggest trying the next exercise with your co-parent. I use this exercise with couples and individuals looking for a clear sense of closure.

Say Goodbye, So You Can Say Hello

You can do this exercise alone by writing your responses in your journal. However, if your co-parent is willing, it can be more effective if you do it together. If it feels comfortable, look each other in the eye and speak directly to each other. Alternatively, you can each write down your responses and share them afterward. Be specific. Feel free to add to this list or to choose only those statements that are relevant to you.

Write or speak the following:

- "Goodbye to everything that made us a romantic couple." Be specific and say goodbye to sex, validation, intimacy, or whatever defined you as a romantic couple.

- "Goodbye to the expectation of getting my emotional and attachment needs met by [say ex's name]."

- "Goodbye to the love that has shifted or is lost."

- "Goodbye to the ways [say ex's name] made me angry, hurt, or sad."

- "Goodbye to taking on or trying to fix my co-parent's emotions."

- "Goodbye to the ways I tried to change myself or [say ex's name] to make it work."

- "Goodbye, [say ex's name]."

Now, say this to yourself (or to your co-parent if you are doing this together):

- "Hello, co-parent!"

- "Hello to the parenting qualities I appreciate about my co-parent."

- "Hello to [say your child's name]'s parent."

- "Hello to our co-parenting relationship."

Shake hands, high-five, or make whatever gesture feels right in the moment.

Now, that you've made a clean break, the best way to establish a strong foundation for your new two-home family is to formally commit to being your kid's co-parents.

Make a Foundational Agreement

This step involves agreeing to set up a two-home structure with your co-parent to guide your teamwork and help you maintain focus on what's best for your kid while also respecting healthy boundaries. You will make many other agreements along the way that cover the specifics of how you co-parent together, but look at this first one as the groundwork for future agreements. Co-parenting teamwork may look different, depending on your circumstances and the needs and age of your kid. Some agreements may need to be revisited as your kid moves through different developmental stages. And the specific arrangements may not always be fifty-fifty. However, your foundational agreement is what your two-home family structure is built upon, so it must be mutually agreed on and solid. If either of you ever feels one of you is wavering from it, it's time to revisit the agreement.

Say Yes

This exercise will work well if you and your co-parent first think about and answer these questions for yourselves individually, and then get together and discuss them. Feel free to change the wording or add your own questions.

- Do you say yes to putting your child's needs first?

- Do you say yes to your child having two present, available, and loving parents?

- Do you say yes to sharing the responsibility of parenting?

- Do you say yes to never threatening the relationship between your child and their other parent?

- Do you say yes to providing a safe harbor for your child?

- Do you say yes to being available to your co-parent as their go-to person as pertains to your child?

- Do you say yes to continuing to be one family for your child in two homes?

- Do you say yes to actively working on and maintaining this co-parenting team?

- Do you say yes to developing a parenting plan that outlines agreements you will both follow through on?

Now come up with one sentence that summarizes your collective yes. This is your foundational agreement, and it will help to put it in writing. For example, "We commit to communicating and working together, so we can both be available and present for [enter your child's name], and keeping their needs front and center." Have fun and don't be afraid to make it personal and unique for your family. Consider making copies that you both sign. Keep it handy. You'll be referring to it all the time!

Now, having made a commitment with your co-parent, you need to regularly attend to it to make sure it stays vital and relevant.

Tend to Your Commitment

Much like a garden, your co-parenting commitment needs regular tending over the months and years. Plants will die without watering and weeding; similarly, you and your co-parent need to find ways to check in, so your co-parenting team stays alive and healthy. It's normal to occasionally lose sight of the fact that your kid is now at the top of your co-parenting triangle. Exciting new elements will enter your life—such as a new partner or a new baby—which may disrupt your other priorities. This may cause the foundation of your triangle to wobble. Or you may struggle at times to balance your own needs, the various needs of a new relationship, and the needs of your child. None of this means you are a bad co-parent or are failing your kid. It's completely natural for outside elements to cause shifts and disruptions. Being aware and prepared is what's key.

I recommend having periodic conversations with your co-parent to help both of you refresh your commitment to co-parenting and putting your child at the top of the triangle. These conversations can cover the following:

- Revisit the *yes* agreements you made in the prior exercise, both to yourself and to your co-parent.

- Revitalize and refresh your commitment by adding to your *yes* list.

- Discuss what's working and what's not working in your co-parenting team.

- Discuss any adjustments that may be needed as a result of your child's changing needs.

- Identify what has caused or might cause you to lose focus in your commitment (such as changes in either of your lives).

Sometimes conversations will be needed to deal with a pressing issue in the moment, such as the perception that one of you is not holding to your commitment. However, don't wait for trouble to arise. That's like waiting until all the plants in your garden droop before you water them. The best way to maintain your co-parenting team is to check in regularly. That way, when issues arise, your team will be solid enough to handle them.

Let's see how Gabriel and Kate are faring now that they've made a clean break, articulated a foundational agreement to commit, and begun to tend to that commitment.

Revisiting Gabriel and Kate

"Our teacher conference is this afternoon," Gabriel reminds Kate on the phone after he drops off their daughter at school. "Are we still good for our preconference meeting now to get some questions together?"

"Thanks for the reminder. I totally forgot!" Kate says a bit distractedly. "Let me put the baby in his stroller. Then I'll be all ears."

Gabriel waits patiently, listening to the baby gurgle as he settles into his stroller. When Kate is back, he continues, "Did you have a chance to read the email from Lilly's teacher? He wants to talk to us about why her grades have fallen."

"Oh gosh!" Kate lets out a sigh. "I haven't had a chance to read it. I didn't realize there was a problem. I mean, Lilly's always welcome to ask me for help with her homework."

"*Maybe you need to ask her more directly,*" Gabriel says, resisting the inclination to criticize Kate's lack of involvement. Then he adds, "*I wonder if something else is going on for her?*"

Kate is quiet for a moment. She feels safe with Gabriel's open-ended question. "*Now that you mention it, I think she's been more withdrawn since the baby was born.*"

"*Yeah, it can be tough on a kid to have a new baby enter the mix so soon after their parents break up. I was mad at my mom when my brother arrived. It took a while to adjust,*" Gabriel says.

"*Good point. I'll ask Dane to take the baby tonight, so Lilly and I can have a mommy-daughter dinner.*"

"*Sounds great. We got sidetracked, though…*" Gabriel laughs.

"*Yeah, we were going to discuss questions for the teacher,*" Kate says, beating him to the thought. "*Let's do that now. Got any ideas?*"

In this scenario, we see evidence of the co-parents' commitment to working together. (They've also each worked on their responses to each other, using the exercises in chapters 2 and 3.) Even if Gabriel is initially frustrated with Kate's forgetfulness, he checks his reaction and responds with patience. Because these two have agreed to work as a team, when an issue comes up, they don't have to restart at zero and convince each other to prioritize the needs of their child. It is understood they both care about her education, will attend teacher conferences, and even get together to plan questions ahead of meeting the teacher. Their foundational agreement also makes it possible for them to discuss more sensitive issues, such as how their daughter feels about a new baby in her family, without becoming defensive. They are flexible and willing to work together to find solutions to help their daughter succeed.

● ● Now What? ● ●

Question: "Are you saying I should be friends with my co-parent?"

Answer: Being friends isn't a prerequisite for co-parenting. You may have seen the smiling faces of separated parents on social media still being besties, with their new partners and all the kids in tow. Or you may have seen your divorced friends go on vacation together. That's all good, but it's not necessary for cooperative co-parenting. You and your co-parent can operate in a respectful way, being amicable but not friends. You can be a committed team without sharing a social life.

Question: "What kind of certainty should my child expect to receive from us as co-parents?"

Answer: Your child needs to feel certain they are loved and cared for by both of you and feel certain they won't lose either of you as a result of your breakup. When I speak about certainty, I'm referring to the secure attachment you and your co-parent need to create for your child. You want to help them feel secure even when their environment is full of change. Your child needs to know they can count on both of you being there for them and following through on what you say you will do. If this certainty is absent, insecurities, fears, anxiety, depression, and other issues can develop.

Question: "What should I do if I'm more committed than my co-parent?"

Answer: You may find that you and your co-parent have different degrees of commitment or ways of showing it. All you can really control is how you choose to commit to your co-parenting responsibilities. Your commitment doesn't depend on whether your co-parent meets you halfway or acts the way you'd like them to. Even if you seem more committed, that's okay. Your child will benefit from your commitment, regardless. How each of you chooses to commit to your co-parenting team sets the stage for your ability to collaborate on all aspects of co-parenting, as we will see in the next chapter.

Chapter 5

Getting on the Same Page

"Are you kidding me?" Sammy says. She and Lukas are having a check-in meeting about their ten-year-old daughter Lane over the phone. "You took her to church? But you're not even religious!"

"I am now," Lukas says. "It's an important part of my life. Plus I want to teach Lane more discipline. You let her walk all over you."

"Geez, I don't recognize you anymore." Sammy recalls discussing religion with Lukas when they decided to have a child. Neither practiced a religion, so they had agreed not to incorporate that into their parenting. She still held that value, but apparently Lukas's values had shifted. "And I don't let her walk all over me," Sammy added. "I respect her opinions."

Lukas pushes back hard. "My religion is my business. I have every right to practice it with my child. Got that? And you wonder why she talks back to you all the time and not to me?"

Sammy feels the familiar rise of anxiety that happens whenever she feels out of control. Lukas's strictness has been a major bone of contention. And now this? She wonders what she can do to steer Lane away from more involvement with religion. Most of all, she worries about the confusion

Lane must feel now that she's stuck in the middle of her parents' conflicting values and parenting styles.

A Collaborative Co-Parenting Vision

Getting on the same page, even with different parenting values and styles, is essential for your co-parenting team to succeed. Winning sports teams and successful work-related teams bring together individuals with vastly different personal values and styles of playing or working, but that doesn't hold them back. Their success comes from their ability to focus on a united goal, despite their differences. Similarly, to be successful co-parents, you need to make united decisions that meet the needs of your child.

In the last chapter, you committed to working as a co-parenting team. Now you will build on that commitment by exploring the second principle of engagement, which is *collaboration*: co-parents collaborate and work together, with a shared vision for co-parenting, to create win-wins for all. You will envision the basis of your collaboration as it pertains to co-parenting: clarifying your values, understanding your parenting styles, building a common vision, and creating a collaborative narrative for your two-home family. Collaboration will help you create a secure and cooperative co-parenting team, so your child can feel safe knowing the two of you are working together.

Much as organizations create vision statements to underlie their daily activities, co-parents benefit from having a common vision they can revisit. This set of co-parenting collaborative values will guide you through difficult moments and decisions and guarantee you keep your child at the top of the triangle. Your collaborative vision will also guide how you choose to parent in your respective homes.

What you each bring to the task of building a collaborative vision are your values and your parenting style.

Clarifying Your Values

Values can be defined as the beliefs that guide who you want to be and how you want to behave. We each have our own values, and any two people bring their respective values to the table. Shared values can motivate two people to become a couple, and conflicting values often contribute to breakups. Perhaps you and your ex experienced values as the major sticking point that landed you in a divorce. Or, like Sammy and Lukas, your value differences may have surfaced only after your breakup.

Our values come from many different sources in our lives, such as school, peers, societal messaging, and social media, as well as from our extended family and the culture we grew up in. Often we adhere to values without consciously choosing them. There are no right or wrong values, and value systems can change over the years. For example, the value of a two-parent, heteronormative nuclear family as the best structure for raising children has shifted; now many people also value families with two homes, single-parent families, foster families, families with same-sex couples, child-free families, blended families, and other alternative family structures.

You may find that some of your values conflict with one or another circumstance in your life. For example, the mere act of getting a divorce may threaten the value system you grew up with. You may also find some of your values conflict with your co-parent's values. Identifying a set of values you and your co-parent both support will remove unnecessary conflict from your child's life. However, even if you and your co-parent present a unified vision, your child may learn some different values in each home.

The process described here will help you reflect on your beliefs, the uniqueness you bring to your family situation, what you want to teach your child, and how you want to show up as a co-parent. These values are yours, not your extended family's or your friends' values, and need not be based on traditional cultural norms. You will probably revisit them often along your co-parenting journey, especially as your child starts to clarify their own values.

What Are Your Co-Parenting Values?

Use this exercise to clarify your values specifically related to co-parenting. If possible, ask your co-parent to do the same. Find a quiet moment to sit by yourself and compile a list of the values you want to embody as a co-parent.

Here are some common core values you may want to include, but don't let this list limit you:

Honesty	Compassion	Respect
Presence	Authenticity	Open-mindedness
Independence	Curiosity	Equality
Kindness	Empathy	Creativity
Responsibility	Teamwork	Flexibility

Write down five to ten value statements describing how you'd like your co-parenting to reflect your values. You may wish to organize your statements according to common parenting categories (such as education or discipline). Here are some examples:

- **Emotional or physical health:** "I value being present for my child's feelings." "It's important my child exercises or plays outdoors regularly."

- **Religion or spirituality:** "It is important for my child to attend temple." "Mindfulness is a valuable practice in my life."

- **Discipline:** "It is important for my child to learn through reasonable consequences." "I favor strictness as a means to teach responsibility."

- **Education:** "I value the cultivation of curiosity." "Being open-minded is crucial to me."

- **Relationships:** "Being respectful is important." "I appreciate having an extended family."

Words such as "value," "important," and "appreciate" help clarify your value statements.

Later, you can share your list of values and value statements with your co-parent and use them to build a collaborative vision. But first let's look at how your values show up in the way you choose to parent.

Understanding Parenting Styles

We don't usually get formal training on how to parent. Nevertheless, our parenting style doesn't come out of nowhere; it reflects our value system, our attachment style, and the parenting we received in our own childhood. As a parent, you may want to replicate what you learned, or you may want to do things differently.

Awareness of your attachment style can shed light on how you respond in relationships; similarly, knowing your parenting style can help you make choices about how to co-parent. It can help you and your co-parent collaborate, even if your styles differ. This, in turn, will help your child feel less confused and anxious and more secure in the continuity between their two homes.

Let's look at three parenting styles that were initially described by Diana Baumrind (1989)—authoritative, authoritarian, and permissive—and at how these parenting styles affect children (Kuppens and Ceulemans 2019). As you read about these styles, consider which most resembles your own or the one you aspire to. Then do the same for your co-parent's style of parenting.

AUTHORITATIVE PARENTING STYLE

- Parent is sensitive, warm, and attuned to their child's emotional and physical needs.

- Parent sets limits, is responsive, and holds boundaries that are fair and appropriate to the situation.

- Parent values listening and allows their child to explore the world.

- Parent may tend toward secure attachment.

- Child tends to be confident, independent, resilient, emotionally balanced, and successful in school and with peers.

AUTHORITARIAN PARENTING STYLE

- Parent is fearful, makes threats, yells, uses punitive measures of discipline.

- Parent makes rigid rules that are not explained to the child.

- Parent places a high value on obedience and maintaining status.

- Parent may tend toward avoidant attachment.

- Child tends to have low self-esteem; hide emotions; be rebellious, aggressive, or anxious; struggle in school and with peers.

PERMISSIVE PARENTING STYLE

- Parent is nurturing, warm, and egalitarian but can seem unconcerned.

- Parent has difficulty with or does not want to provide structure or set boundaries and limits.

- Parent may fear disappointing or not being liked by their child.

- Parent may tend toward either secure or ambivalent attachment.

- Child tends to be creative and resourceful but can have low self-reliance; be impulsive, domineering, or anxious; and struggle with social skills or authority.

Going back to the example of Sammy and Lukas, his belief in strict discipline suggests an authoritarian parenting style. His accusation that Sammy lets their daughter "walk all over" her indicates he sees her as too permissive. Sammy, on the other hand, stresses respecting Lane's opinions, indicating the positive qualities of a permissive or authoritative style.

Some research suggests that your parenting style may reflect your attachment style. For example, parents who use an authoritative style tend to have secure attachment (Doinita and Nijloveanu 2015). However, any parenting style that helps a child feels safe, seen, and secure will foster secure attachment with their parent. I suggest using this information to become more aware of your own and your co-parent's styles and to have compassionate conversations about how you choose to parent between your two homes.

Some variation in your own and your co-parent's styles of parenting is okay and normal, as long as your child doesn't perceive conflict over the differences or feel they've been put in the middle of a parental dispute. Clarifying your respective parenting styles in a cordial manner will help you build a collaboration that prioritizes your child's needs. Regardless of your differences and what happened between you in the past, you both are and will always be your kid's parents.

Creating a Shared Vision

Now that you have thought about your co-parenting values and parenting style, and those of your co-parent, it's time to build common ground. You're going to come up with a common vision. The goal is to do this together with your co-parent, as a first step in your collaboration. I understand that not all co-parents will be equally receptive. If your co-parent doesn't wish to participate, you can modify this process to do on your own.

Some co-parents find that they share the same values, much as they did when they first got together. If this is the case, you'll find the following exercise easy. However, in my experience, it is more common for co-parents to have at least some divergent values and to have somewhat different parenting styles. The intention here is to create a vision that is broad enough to incorporate the values and styles of both parents. Again, your child may learn some different values and habits in each home, and that's okay.

What Is Your Shared Co-Parenting Vision?

Sit down with your co-parent to talk about your common vision for co-parenting. Ideally, your co-parent will have already taken time to think about their own values and parenting style.

1. Share your value statements and parenting styles. This could be a fully open sharing or a more limited discussion if that's more comfortable.

2. Acknowledge your differences. Agree that it's okay to have differences. Examine where they originated: what did you learn in your respective families and backgrounds?

3. Identify your common ground. Look for any areas of agreement.

4. Create a shared vision. Formulate a list of statements you and your co-parent can agree on to guide your collaboration. I suggest making it brief, maybe three to ten statements.

You will be referring to this shared vision throughout your co-parenting journey.

Here are some statements my co-parent and I included in our shared vision:

- "We respect and honor Ellie's relationship with her other parent."

- "Ellie deserves to be free from the burdens of our conflicts and disagreements."

- "We will make sure that Ellie's voice, feelings, wants, and emotions are heard and valued."

- "We value our differences in perspective and skill sets and see them as opportunities for Ellie to gain more diversity of thoughts and skills."

- "We will teach Ellie to be honest, empathetic, open, and curious to learn."

To complete our discussion about building a common vision, let's visit Sammy and Lukas again. This talk occurs after they came up with their shared vision statement.

Revisiting Sammy and Lukas

"I'd like to bring something up," Lukas says. "I know it's a sensitive issue."

"Okay," says Sammy, feeling a wave of old anxiety but also wanting to trust their new process.

"I'm planning to take Lane to church this weekend."

"All right." Sammy pauses. "I appreciate the heads-up."

"I know this is hard for you—"

"It is," Sammy says quickly. "I get that religion is important to you now. I also get that since we're no longer together, what you do is your business. Still, I think it's important to be on the same page about how we discuss this with Lane."

"Agreed!"

"I had to dig deep on this," Sammy continues. "I remembered a value we talked about early on: wanting our kid to be open-minded and curious about new things. Maybe we can center around that now?"

"I like it," Lukas says. "I realize she'll hear a different perspective on religion from you. You've never been one not to share your ideas! Plus you'll probably let her watch—what's that show called?—that she can't see at my house."

They laugh together.

Sammy is quiet, gathering her thoughts. "How can we make sure Lane doesn't feel confused when she goes to church with you? We don't want her to feel torn."

"Good point," Lukas says, "I think we let her know we've talked about it, and sometimes people have different beliefs, and that's okay. We want her to be open to different beliefs."

After identifying that they both value open-mindedness and curiosity, Sammy and Lukas were able to accept that they will be discussing religion from different perspectives with their daughter. They will do so without undermining the other parent's beliefs. They are also willing to tolerate some variance in their respective parenting styles. Their priority is to keep Lane out of an ideological war and instead to strengthen their collaborative vision for co-parenting. They will each have interesting conversations with their child, which will allow her to create her own value system and choices around spirituality. In this way, they are building a shared vision that is broad enough and respectful enough to incorporate both their perspectives and to create a new narrative for their two-home family.

Creating a Collaborative Narrative

Separation and divorce are not one-time events for your child, but an ongoing experience. One way to support your child through this experience is for you and your co-parent to collaborate on a new family story that is not about a family breaking up but about a family changing.

No two children respond in the same way to the news of their parents' breakup, even in the same household. But in the absence of constructive conversations, children tend to come up with fantasies that put them at the center of the action. They may fault themselves or feel they have the power to bring you back together. If you try to protect them from whatever they're feeling, they may feel they have to hide those feelings. Instead, you and your co-parent can share a narrative that makes it clear to your child that their grief, sadness, anger, fear, confusion, questions, and experiences are all part of their family story, and that's okay. At first, your child may not understand that their family can still be a family, but they will feel more secure knowing their feelings are welcome and that their parents are working collaboratively, even in two homes.

To create a collaborative story, you and your co-parent want to provide a unified and neutral explanation for your breakup. This doesn't mean you have to tell the whole truth and nothing but the truth. It's better to leave out exactly who did what and other gory details. Agree to focus on the commonalities of your shared vision and the joy your child has brought you both. Keep your story short, clear, unified, and free of blame. Don't use it to play tug-of-war with your child's allegiances. A collaborative narrative provides your child with an empowering family story that includes them, as opposed to two separate narratives that may conflict.

If your breakup took place some time ago, you and your co-parent likely have already talked with your child about it. However, it's not too late to revisit that conversation in a more collaborative manner. Your child's perspective on how their family story evolves over time will be part of their healing journey.

Your New Family Story

Ideally, you and your co-parent will sit down together with your child as soon as you've figured out the logistical details of your breakup that will have a direct impact on them. It is good to have this conversation after you and your co-parent have gotten on the same page with a collaborative vision.

1. Find a quiet place where you can talk without being interrupted.

2. Discuss your breakup. If it happened some time ago, you can introduce the discussion by saying you'd like to have a more complete, open conversation. Provide reasons that are age appropriate and will make sense to your child. Stress your unified narrative. For example say, "We both feel..." "We decided..." "Things changed between us." "We're both sad." "We were

fighting too much, so we agreed it would be better not to live together."

3. Reassure your child. Explain that your love for your child will never end or change and that the breakup was not their fault but was due to adult issues they can't fix. Clarify that you both will still be their parents forever, and they can continue to rely on you both to be there for them and keep them safe.

4. Discuss your new family structure. Review with your child what will change and what won't. Be specific. For example, say, "Now you have two homes, one with each parent. Your other home is only fifteen minutes away. You'll stay in the same school and can see your friends at both homes."

5. Give your child a voice. Acknowledge, listen to, and validate your child's emotions. Answer any questions in a way that doesn't favor one parent over the other. Make sure your child feels part of—not the cause of—the new family story. Include them in decisions that are appropriate, such as setting up their new room and naming each house. Giving your child a voice can happen throughout the discussion, but be sure to end the conversation with it.

You can revisit your family story over time, as your child asks more questions and seeks new information. Continue to discuss their feelings, what they enjoy about their two homes, what is unique and special about each one, and any struggles they may have. Talking openly and normalizing their family story will help to reduce any shame or discomfort they may experience. As long as you and your co-parent stay on the same page and avoid blame, your child can have these subsequent discussions with either of you. How you talk about separation and divorce and how you integrate it into the fabric of your family story will help your child feel more secure and empowered moving forward.

Collaboration may take time to develop. But if you keep working at it, it can become the cornerstone of a secure foundation for your two-home family. Your collaborative family narrative can be a throughline that expands and shifts through the years, as you and your child add chapters to it. As we will see in the next chapter, developing clear and secure ways to communicate and make decisions together as co-parents will support your commitment to functioning as a team.

● ● Now What? ● ●

Question: "Can co-parents' attachment styles affect their ability to come up with a shared vision?"

Answer: Yes, your attachment style can make it easier or harder to collaborate. If you have avoidant tendencies, collaboration may feel threatening. You may come to the table with everything figured out, knowing how you want it to be. If your co-parent offers a different perspective, you may take that as an attack or criticism and become defensive. If you have ambivalent tendencies, you welcome collaboration, but if your co-parent doesn't meet you halfway, you may get anxious or angry. If you have secure attachment, you welcome collaboration but also are open to dialogue and the give-and-take necessary to arrive at a shared vision.

Question: "Will growing up with different values in two homes harm my child later in life?"

Answer: No. As your child moves into the preteen and teen years, they'll develop their own values. Having some divergent values in your respective homes creates teachable moments for your child and the opportunity to develop critical thinking skills and to learn how to make their own value-based choices. The goal is for your child to experience secure attachment with both co-parents, so make sure you don't devalue your co-parent or push your values as better or right.

Question: "My kid's dad is super strict. How can I make up for that at my house?"

Answer: I understand you want to protect your child, and it can be hard to see your co-parent act in ways that conflict with your parenting style. If the two of you can't find a middle ground, however, trying to compensate by being overly permissive won't help. Creating extremes will only confuse your child, and letting them run the show may make it harder for them to relate to others or develop secure attachment. Instead, setting appropriate boundaries and limits in your own home will create a structure your child can rely on to feel safe, even if it's only in one household.

Chapter 6

Communicating Without Conflict

My co-parent and I had to work hard to get to a place where we could communicate with clarity. Initially, we had no guidelines to follow. We didn't know how to make requests of each other or discuss parenting decisions without an emotional charge. All this came to a head one morning when my co-parent arrived to pick up Ellie. I was cajoling her to finish brushing her teeth, when he blurted out, "By the way, I'm taking Ellie to Colorado the first week of August to visit friends."

I felt a quick squeeze of anxiety in my gut. He was presenting his request as a done deal when it was something we needed to discuss. And now that Ellie had heard, how could I say no? I wheeled around and mouthed that now wasn't the time to resolve this. Then I rushed into the kitchen.

He followed. "What are you doing? We don't have secrets from Ellie," he said loudly.

Ellie followed as well, her eyes darting back and forth between us. I wanted to smile and wipe away the traces of toothpaste still in the corners of her mouth, but I was immobilized. I could feel the heat rise in the room, as if the furnace had just been turned to 100 degrees. "That's during my time with her," I managed to say. I could hear the snappiness in my voice.

"I've already made plans," he said on his way to the door. "Come on, Ellie, let's go."

She had been ready to go, but suddenly she was hiding in the corner behind the table. She wasn't playing. She was scared, confused. She just wanted it all to stop.

We had thrust our daughter in the middle of our conflict. We were both focused on our own needs: I wanted to preserve what I saw as my time, and her dad was making his plans. We weren't considering Ellie. Instead, what we needed to do was communicate with each other in ways that prevented conflict from arising in the first place.

You may think that's a tall order. Conflict is to be expected in two-home families, right? It's a given in your life, no? You may feel frustrated about not being heard or understood by your co-parent or may want them to see that you know better than they do about what your kid needs. You may find yourself thinking "It's like we're on different planets. If there is some secret sauce for communication, I missed it along the way." You may wish you had a pull-down menu every time you interacted to help you say the right thing. But even if you manage to say the right thing, you can't predict how your co-parent will respond. Or can you?

In fact, it is probably more possible than you realize to get a handle on communications with your co-parent. In this chapter, we will dive into the principle of *clarity*: co-parents maintain clear, concise, calm, and timely communications, thereby minimizing misunderstandings and conflict. With greater clarity, you can move out of the foggy landscape of assumptions and expectations, and toward greater trust and collaboration, so you don't put your child in the middle. We will begin by looking at how your attachment style influences both how you communicate and how you receive communications. You'll learn some skills to improve two kinds of communication that come up frequently between co-parents: making requests and decision-making. I will describe a simple decision-making process that can keep you and your co-parent out of the conflict zone.

Finally, we'll look at how you can communicate if conflict does arise between you and your co-parent.

Communication and Attachment Style

By now, you have a pretty good idea of what attachment styles you and your co-parent have. Those styles reflect the communication patterns you saw in your families of origin. Think back to how your parents or primary caretakers responded when you expressed an emotion or need. Did they listen and respond in helpful ways? Did you witness loud discussions or feel the silence of we-don't-talk-about-it disagreements? As you got older, was the door open to talk about whatever you were going through, or did communications have to be brief and unemotional? Did you have to manage your caregivers' emotions to maintain connection?

Recognizing the communication patterns you and your co-parent use can help you take the hot potatoes out of your interactions. In other words, you can learn to separate your respective stuff from the actual information being exchanged. In my case, that would have entailed recognizing that my co-parent's avoidant attachment predisposed him to create a plan on his own and then inform me about it. I also would have had to recognize my ambivalent tendency to feel out of control when I don't think I've been included in a decision. Working together or asking questions didn't factor in for either of us.

Let's look at the communication patterns typical for each attachment style, including general delivery and response patterns and what the person needs to feel comfortable with communication. Some patterns can be either helpful or a hindrance, depending on the situation. For example, the avoidant tendency not to express much emotion can work in business settings; however, not expressing feelings can make it hard to stay connected in personal settings. Here, we'll look at patterns as they apply specifically to co-parenting communications.

Avoidant Communication Patterns

As someone with avoidant attachment, you tend to offer few or no details when providing information to your co-parent. You don't mention emotions, such as how something made you feel. You like to feel independent and trusted, so you make unilateral decisions and don't leave room for input or back-and-forth discussion. Your communications can sound a little rigid and inflexible, even cold. You may prefer to use definitive statements—such as a quick "I've got it handled" or "I'm fine"—rather than questions.

Your emails and texts are infrequent, with few words. You may ghost or forget to respond.

If you feel overwhelmed or pressured during an interaction, you may not respond or may even walk out. If you feel criticized, you may lash back with blame or accusations of your own, because coming off as incapable or wrong feels unsafe for you. You try to convince instead of stating a need. Asking for help or input doesn't come easily. When input sounds like you're being told what to do, you may shut it down or get defensive.

You respond better to communications with your co-parent when you have time to process beforehand and have a time frame for when your co-parent needs a response. You like things brief and to the point and presented in a neutral, not overly emotional, tone.

Ambivalent Communication Patterns

As someone with ambivalent attachment, you tend to use emotionally charged words and provide lots of detail when speaking with your co-parent. You often respond immediately, before processing your thoughts and emotions. You may repeat yourself if you feel your co-parent hasn't heard you or try to discuss multiple issues at once. You may bring up tangential information or things from the past that aren't relevant to your co-parenting relationship.

Your texts and emails tend to be detailed, verbose, and frequent, especially if your co-parent is not responding.

You bring a sense of urgency to discussions and may get anxious or angry if your co-parent isn't equally engaged or doesn't respond quickly. You may say things to either placate or punish your co-parent, even if you don't mean it. You may also roll your eyes, catastrophize, or make threats. If conflict arises, you prefer to work through it in the moment. Waiting for a response is hard for you and creates anxiety and overthinking.

You respond well to communications with your co-parent when you feel you're getting all the facts and relevant info in a timely manner. If your co-parent can't respond immediately, you appreciate having a time frame. You like to feel included so you know what to expect.

Secure Communication Patterns

As someone with secure attachment, you provide information to your co-parent in a timely fashion and with sufficient detail. When you don't have information to share or are unavailable to deliver it, you're clear about that. You are comfortable letting your co-parent know how you feel, without using blame or shame. Your communications are friendly and respectful.

You use emails and texts as a natural extension of in-person communications and are sensitive to the appropriate number and frequency of messages.

You are able to separate your feelings from the issues. You listen to and consider your co-parent's perspective, without feeling threatened or anxious, and can feel empathy for different points of views. You bring curiosity to a conversation and are open to dialoguing about solutions. You own your part in any conflict, while also expressing your concerns clearly and concisely.

Your communications with your co-parent take into consideration both of your needs in a clear, open, and transparent manner. You use language that acknowledges the other person and shows appreciation. You want communication to focus on observations, not assumptions, and on solutions rather than emotions. You can hold your own boundaries and limits while respecting those of the other: "No, I can't talk now. How about 8:00 p.m.?" Or "Yes, you can take kiddo this weekend. But let's do a trade."

Now that you've seen how attachment styles influence communication, let's put this into action so you and your co-parent can move toward more secure communication and greater clarity.

Moving Toward Secure

Even if you don't have secure attachment, you can use this exercise to create secure communication between you and your co-parent. You can do this exercise alone, or you and your co-parent can do it together.

1. Review the communication patterns for your co-parent's attachment style, paying particular attention to what someone with that style responds well to. Identify one pattern you feel is typical of your co-parent.

2. Pick one way you can change to address that pattern. For example, asking "What do you think?" can speak both to the person with avoidant attachment, who may not like to be told what to do, and to the person with ambivalent attachment, who wants to feel included. When discussing day care options, you might say, "I think this would be a good option. What do you think?" Or "Let me know when you can discuss options. I'm interested in your thoughts."

3. Try out your new way of communicating with your co-parent in real time. Notice the changes.

4. Now identify one pattern you feel is typical of *you*. Come up with a way to change your pattern when speaking with your co-parent that would work better for both of you. For example, if you have ambivalent attachment, instead of waiting or demanding, you might ask your co-parent, "Could you please email all the information about the orientation by tomorrow? Thanks!" Or if you have avoidant tendencies, instead of ignoring your

co-parent, you might say, "Sorry, I won't have time. I'll send it to you this weekend."

5. Try out this new way of communicating with your co-parent in real time. Notice the impact.

If you and your co-parent are doing this exercise together, discuss how your new ways of communicating worked for each of you. Did you feel heard? Did you each get your needs met?

As you move toward secure communication, watch for patterns that reflect your or your co-parent's attachment styles. For example, if you notice one of you talking with charged emotion, that could be a sign of ambivalent attachment. In that case, name it—silently to yourself—and adjust accordingly.

Getting to Clarity

Communicating in a secure way may not always be easy, but it's a muscle you and your co-parent can build with practice even if you didn't grow up with secure communication patterns. For secure communication— including the ability to think clearly, make sound decisions, and communicate calmly and empathetically—your upstairs brain needs to regulate your emotions, so your downstairs brain isn't running the show. If you can do this, you'll find communications taking a giant leap forward. You can also do this with your child to maintain connection and to help them develop secure attachment—both with you and in their relationships moving forward.

The following five guidelines can help you work toward secure communication and greater clarity with your co-parent. The beauty of these guidelines is that they work well for co-parents with avoidant or ambivalent tendencies, because they help you nip either of those tendencies in the bud. If you follow these guidelines, you increase your chances of not triggering your co-parent and not becoming triggered yourself.

Be Considerate and Respectful

If you and your co-parent aren't starting with a base of consideration (being thoughtful) and respect (valuing each other), it will be hard to achieve secure communication. When you were a couple, the glue that held you together was your love for each other. Now that you've moved on, that glue must be respect for your child's other parent. One easy way to show respect is through appreciation of your wins. For example, you might say, "It was really helpful that you packed Tim's clothes for his school trip." Or "I appreciated your reminder." Or "Thanks for switching our parenting days." Or "High-five to an awesome birthday party." A co-parent who's been appreciated will feel seen and valued rather than think, "What's the point? They never notice anyway."

Be Brief and Concise

When communicating with your co-parent, less is often more. It can be helpful to discuss which forms of communication you each prefer to use. Keep your texts and emails short and clear. In written communication, bullet points are your friend. Keep phone calls to a few minutes. For longer discussions and regularly scheduled check-ins—in person, on the phone, or online—or if you are doing exercises from this book together, set clear times to begin and end your meeting. This will help you maintain boundaries.

Provide Relevant Information

Stay focused on the facts. Avoid emotional content, blaming, or critical language. Keep your communication focused on your child. If you're making a request, back it up with any information your co-parent will need. Use neutral language. Making simple, factual observations will keep defensiveness at bay. For example, don't say, "I need you to pick up Clara on time. She says you're always late." Instead, simply say, "I'm checking in about pick-up time for Clara's band practice. It's at 3:00 p.m. Could you let her know if you're running late?" Similarly, don't say, "You should give Ahmed food he likes. He's not eating anything." Instead, you can say, "I've noticed Ahmed isn't eating much of his lunch. Let's talk about a meal plan for him."

Ask Questions

If you don't have enough information about your co-parent's request, ask clarifying questions instead of making assumptions, being reactive, or getting defensive to a perceived criticism. For example, if your co-parent is taking your child on a car trip, rather than freaking out at the assumption your child will be buckled into a car seat for five hours, ask, "How often will you stop along the way?" This will put you on the same team as your co-parent, not pit you against each other.

Asking questions shows your co-parent that you value their input. It promotes the feeling of choice and builds a sense of trust and collaboration. It also decreases the chance that you will get a negative response. For example, your co-parent is not likely to respond well if you say, "I told my parents we are meeting them at the airport on Thursday. So I have to pick up kiddo a day early." Try this instead: "My parents are arriving on Thursday. Would it be okay if I pick up kiddo a day early so we can meet them together?"

Roger That

Respond to your co-parent's texts or emails within an appropriate amount of time. Acknowledge you received and understood the message. A simple thumbs-up emoji or "got it" will do wonders to maintain secure communication. If you can't meet or can't answer a request because you're too busy or overwhelmed, let your co-parent know when you can. Be specific ("I'll get back to you by 3:30 today"). Similarly, let your co-parent know when you need an answer ("The deadline to sign up for swim classes is October 1. Please let me know by September 28, so I can submit the application"). Also, let your co-parent know about any changes in plans ahead of time. For example, "I have a work trip the first week of October. Could you keep kiddo those extra days? We could do a trade." Rarely do people react well to surprises (unless it's a party!).

Set Your Team Up for Success

Discuss this series of questions with your co-parent to create a framework for managing your ongoing communications.

1. What platform works best for secure and clear communication between you, and in which situations? For example, does email, texting, a parenting app, or in-person contact work best for you?

2. How often will you communicate about updates and changes regarding your child? What issues and topics do you want to be updated on regularly?

3. What is an appropriate response time?

4. How would you like to acknowledge the receipt of information?

5. How will you each be alerted in the event of an urgent matter?

6. How will you communicate in front of your child?

This framework for communication will help you stay focused on your child.

One key element to secure communication is a sense of mutuality. Understanding your respective attachment styles and how to work with each other's communication needs can set you up for win-wins in which you both gain the clarity you need and feel respected and understood.

Co-parents often find themselves caught up in misunderstandings and conflict over decision-making. Let's look at how you can function as a team.

Decision-Making and Requests

When the two of you were married, you made important decisions together. That doesn't change in a separated household. Even when bonus (or step) parents enter the picture, the two of you are still the main decision-makers for your child. Your child will feel safe and secure knowing their parents have the big decisions under control and that they don't have to step in and make them for you. They will also appreciate knowing their family's foundation is still intact.

I've found many co-parents work well if they see themselves as a cooperative steering committee for their two-home family. Whether or not you call yourselves a "committee," you can function as one by setting your agenda, scheduling meetings, and following an agreed-upon process. This will ensure that all decisions—including ones that end up in your co-parenting plan (or custody and visitation agreement), if you have one—are focused on your child's needs and personality. Co-parenting plans are often required by the courts to guide a two-home family through the years.

Before getting into the details of the steering committee's functions, let's look at how things are going for June and Angela, who have a decision to make about their son's phone.

June: (texts) Hey, btw, I got James a phone for his birthday!

Angela: (texts back) What? I don't want him having a phone yet.

June: Why not? He's twelve. All his friends have phones.

Angela: This isn't your decision to make.

June: I thought you were on board with techy stuff.

Angela: I am! And I know social media can be harmful. James is too young.

June: He'll be fine. I was just giving you a heads-up, so you don't also get him one.

Angela: I'll get him a phone when I think he's ready.

June: Then he'll have two phones. That's nuts! Plus he'll want to have it at your house.

Angela: Not happening!

June and Angela are trying to make a big decision on the fly, via text, and obviously aren't working together. They're letting their fears and need for control take center stage. As someone with avoidant attachment, June would happily handle the decision on her own. As someone with ambivalent attachment, Angela feels left out and doesn't trust June to make a decision that reflects a common set of values.

Like June and Angela, you and your co-parent share responsibility for discussing and making all major decisions about your child's life together. Regardless of what request or decision is on the table, you need to be able to move through it with ease. Here is a six-step decision-making process built on the principle of secure communication, through which you can find mutually beneficial solutions for your co-parent steering committee. Your child will also benefit, as they won't be stuck in the middle of messy decision-making or feel burdened to make decisions for you.

A Six-Step Decision-Making Process

The following cooperative decision-making process is designed primarily for in-person meetings of your co-parent steering committee, as most important decisions are best made in person. You can use and adapt portions for other decisions made via email or other electronic communications.

As you work with this process, notice which types of decisions lend themselves to in-person dialogue and when written messages can work. The key is finding whatever gets you to your goal in a way that leaves emotions, defensiveness, and finger-pointing out of the process. Coming to the table with a decision already made in your mind, or already discussed with your child, will make it hard to work together. Leave space for input. Notice if your own stuff—your past experiences, fears, anger, or shame, and how you want to be perceived—could affect the outcome. Separating your personal stuff from the problem at hand will help you both stay focused on your child. When co-parents feel their needs, interests, and options have been considered, they're more likely to say yes or find a compromise than to give a hard no (Fisher and Ury 2011). Here are the steps.

1. **The prep.** Let your co-parent know what you'd like to discuss ahead of time. Find a time and place convenient for both of you. Do your research and come prepared with any information needed for the decision at hand. Set an agenda, so you both know what topics are on the table and how much time you need for discussion. I suggest focusing on one topic (two max). You can set up some guidelines to help keep the peace. For example, keep the discussion focused on your child, keep your emotions out of the discussion, remain creative and flexible, be kind and empathetic.

2. **The presentation.** Whoever (co-parent A) requested this agenda item presents the information, needs, research, budget requirements, logistics, and options in a structured and clear way. Stick to the facts. The more relevant details and info, the less room for assumptions. (If you are communicating by email or text, bullet points can work well.) Keep your presentation short and focused on the needs and interests of your child. End by inviting feedback, such as "Fiona is turning three and may benefit from being around other kids at day care. I'm concerned about too much travel time

for her. I'd like to find a place between our houses. What do you think?"

3. **Clarification.** Co-parent B listens before responding and then reflects back what they heard. Co-parent B asks clarifying questions, and co-parent A clarifies what was misunderstood or not covered. Show empathy so your co-parent feels understood. For example, "I hear you saying Fiona may be ready for day care. I understand you're anxious to get back to a regular work schedule but also want time with Fiona. Can you clarify how many hours per week?" Be careful not to move into a counterperspective until all clarification is complete.

4. **Counterperspective.** Co-parent B now has a turn to share their interests, perspective, needs, and options, while co-parent A listens. For example, "I think Fiona could benefit from staying home a bit longer, or if she does go, then only for half days." Then co-parent A reflects what they heard, showing empathy and asking for clarification, if needed. For example, "I hear you think Fiona could benefit from staying at home a bit longer. Help me understand why this is important to you."

5. **Problem solve.** Brainstorm and identify all the options that represent your two perspectives. Identify areas of agreement as well as differing interests. Consider how your options align with your collaborative values (refer to the shared co-parenting vision you created in chapter 5). What are your priorities? Where can you compromise? What is making it hard? How will you share responsibility? What will be the impact on your child now and in the future? Based on your common values and priorities, make your best decision. It can be helpful to see your decision in writing. Send a text or email as a follow-up. I suggest signing it. If you can't come to a mutual decision, consider seeking the help of a mediator or coach. As a last resort, take the matter to court. However, going

to court can be a high-conflict situation, which won't bode well for your child or your pocketbook.

6. **Tell your child together.** Beforehand, discuss how you'll talk with your child about the decision. Regardless of their age, it's important for your child to know you are in agreement. For example, you might say, "Fiona, we want to let you know you'll be going to the preschool we visited last week. We both agreed you will go for three days." Listen to and observe their feelings and leave room for their input. If you think aspects of a decision may be hard for them to hear, find a united way to present those aspects as well.

Let's see how things are different for June and Angela when they attempt to function as a steering committee and follow the decision-making process just outlined.

• June and Angela: Take 2

This time, June and Angela are speaking on the phone instead of by text. June starts by thanking Angela for agreeing to meet. "We've only got one item on the agenda," she says.

"Yes, phones," Angela says. "Why don't you present your ideas first?"

"Okay," June says. "I realize we have different opinions, but I think we should consider James's situation. All his friends have phones, and I don't want to put him at a social disadvantage. He complains he's left out because he doesn't have a phone. Your thoughts?"

Angela tells June she agrees their son's social development is important. "I'm wondering," she says, "did you check research on the effects of social media?"

"No. But we should," June says. "Do you want to share your ideas now?"

Angela smiles. She's one step ahead. "Well, the research results are a mixed bag. Phones help kids get a jump on digital literacy, and they're good in emergencies. But I'm concerned about cyberbullying and access to social media. I want him spending more time outside or doing homework, which we both value."

June asks some clarifying questions about the research, then says, "So am I hearing that you're open to a phone if we take steps to guard against possible problems?"

Angela acknowledges she is. She's confident they can limit James's phone use, so she's comfortable having it in their homes. "Why don't you research which apps are good for tracking, and I'll look up parental controls."

"Sounds good."

"He'll be thrilled," Angela says. "But we didn't discuss which phone and who buys it."

"Good point," June says. "I've already done my shopping. I'll send you details. Maybe this can be a gift from us both."

"I'd like that," Angela says, "especially since his last big gift came from you. Let's give it to him together."

In this scenario, June and Angela follow the structure of the decision-making process by setting a time and agenda, taking turns offering their perspectives, listening and clarifying, and looking at options. They also exemplify secure communication. When Angela starts to feel triggered about inclusion (who will buy the phone), June makes a point of bringing her in. They both use an abundance of *we-statements*, building a collaborative basis for their eventual decision.

You may be wondering if June and Angela should have included James in any part of their discussion. Let's consider this issue.

When to Involve Your Child in Decision-Making

It is helpful to distinguish between adult-led decisions and child-led decisions. Adult-led decisions (like those in table 1) should take into consideration your child's emotional and developmental needs and interests. Parents are in charge of major as well as everyday decision-making for their child.

Table 1. Common Types of Adult-Led Decisions

Major decisions	Day-to-day decisions
Education	Scheduling (medical appointments, extracurricular)
Health care	Diet and exercise
Religion/religious practices	Household responsibilities
Parenting time/living arrangements/custody	Screen time/TV
Sleep routines	Phone use
Finances/child support	Social media
Childcare	How to talk about puberty/sex
Vacations/holidays	Allowance
Discipline and boundaries	Transportation (drop-offs and pick-ups)

June and Angela's discussion about giving a phone to James is a good example of an adult-led decision. James asked for a phone, but it's still up to his co-parents to decide whether he will have one.

As co-parents of an infant or an unborn child, all your decisions will be adult led. That will evolve as your child gets older. For example, a teen will naturally have more say in their living arrangements than a young child will. Make adult-led decisions together with your co-parent before discussing them with your child. If you want to include your child's input, the two of you should discuss that input with your child. Your child needs the safety you provide, as they expand into making decisions for themselves.

Child-led decisions can help your child feel considered and seen, especially during separation and divorce. Your child needs to feel they have some level of control and choice in their lives. Decisions initiated by your child can be about your child's social activities, activities that reflect their interests, or hobbies. When decisions are child led, you still need to work with your co-parent to coordinate scheduling and budgeting, as well as conversations with your child, to ensure follow-through between your two homes. Staying attuned to your child's needs for autonomy and decision-making power will be an ongoing conversation.

Note that child-only decisions, such as those related to gender (including gender expansiveness, gender expression, and how your child wants to identify and their preferred pronouns) and sexual orientation, are ones your child has the right to make for themselves. Getting on team kiddo and understanding and respecting your child's needs and choices is the best way you and your co-parent can help your child feel seen and know they have the support and safety they require.

Clear decision-making can help you avoid conflict. You both walk away feeling heard and understood. The process I described may feel a bit clunky at first, but with practice, you will find it becomes natural. Even so, at times, you may reach an impasse and conflict may arise.

Reframing Conflict to Find Win-Win-Wins

You may view conflict as a lose-lose for everyone. However, in every relationship—including ones between co-parents—some conflict is inevitable. For this reason, rather than striving to avoid all conflict, I prefer to focus on how you handle conflicts that do arise.

In the midst of a conflict, it may feel like you and your co-parent are two adults on a sinking ship with no lifeboat. You're too busy duking it out to notice your child is on board too. In this situation, you have a choice: you can let the ship sink and go down with all of you, or you can work with your co-partner to find dry land.

Fights aren't always loud screaming matches. They can also be like a cold war. Either way, allowing your child to witness the conflict can have a very negative impact. At a neurological level, being put in the middle of parental conflict causes distress to your child, which causes their brain to increase production of the stress hormone cortisol (Davies et al. 2020). This, in turn, is associated with an increased risk of short-term and long-term issues, including depression, anxiety, poor self-esteem, and behavioral issues. For me, the potential for these effects is the number one reason to figure my stuff out and to work on improving communication with my co-parent.

When you were in a romantic relationship with your ex, you probably felt so many things were riding on the positive outcome of a conflict between you. Ultimately, though, conflict-free relationships don't exist, and your future as a couple depended on your ability to fight fairly and to repair quickly. Now you may be thinking, "My ex and I failed at that. That's why we're no longer together, and now you're asking us handle conflict well?"

Not exactly. I'm reminding you that because you're no longer in a romantic relationship, the reasons and rules and expectations around conflict are different, and whatever you fought about before is no longer relevant. What's relevant now is that you and your co-parent collaborate in ways that put the interests and needs of your child first. Conflict is an indication that the attachment cables between you and your co-parent are still entangled and your interpersonal relationship has moved to the top of the triangle, taking priority over your child's needs.

Ideally, understanding how your current relationship is different is enough to let you walk away from conflicts. And sometimes that does happen. You tell yourself, "This is old stuff that doesn't matter anymore." Or, if you need more of a reminder that your co-parent is no longer responsible for meeting your attachment needs, you can use a self-empowerment message. My two favorites are "I'm not going to get roses from a hardware store" and "Just focus on Ellie." When I repeat one of these to myself, I'm able to stop an emotional trigger from taking over. It's no longer about *my* needs. Then I can respond with facts or by choosing to let a comment roll off me, so I can refocus on what's best for my child.

I suggest coming up with your own personal message. Find a phrase you can have handy to help you find your calm. Think of it as your quick reminder of what you know to be true. It can be about your own personal win or the strengths you bring to the co-parenting relationship. Don't hesitate to be creative! Say it out loud, tape it up around your house, have it on your phone. Tell your friends to remind you of it.

It feels good to drop the hot potato and cool off. But I recognize that this isn't always easy to do. There will be times when you find yourself embroiled in a fight with your co-parent because communications have broken down. All the emotional triggers and reactions we discussed in chapters 2 and 3 take over. In that situation, you need to reframe what is happening.

By *reframe*, I mean view the situation in a different way. Reframing co-parental conflict involves shifting away from stuff that originated in your past relationship and shifting into your current roles as co-parents.

At the beginning of this chapter, I described the conflict in which my co-parent announced in front of Ellie that he was taking her to Colorado for a vacation. In the moment, I was unable to reframe the interaction. But here's how I could have done it. I could have said to myself, "Okay, stop reacting." I could have taken a breath and tuned into my body and noticed signs of anxiety. I might have realized I was reacting this way because of times in the past when I felt like I couldn't rely on my ex to provide me with relevant information. I could have used my self-empowerment message: *I can't get roses from the hardware store. Now all that matters is focusing on Ellie's needs.* If I had done all that, my body would have calmed down and my prefrontal cortex would have come back online. Then I could have turned to my co-parent and said, "Thanks for the info about your vacation. Let's chat about it later on the phone."

Reframing in this manner allows for a win-win-win. It's a win for me because I'm able to leap free of my old patterns and triggers. It's a win-win for my co-parent and me because we can refocus on what matters in the moment: our daughter. And remember, it only takes one co-parent making a shift to move both of you away from old dynamics. Finally, it's a win-win-win for Ellie because she doesn't have to be cowering in the corner if her parents are communicating with clarity.

● ● Now What? ● ●

Question: "My co-parent is talking about taking a job in another city. What do I do when they have all the say-so in a major decision?"

Answer: A big decision like this may feel overwhelming because you have no say. Realistically, sometimes a co-parent's needs will overshadow the needs of the child. In this case, your co-parent may need that job for financial reasons. However, your communications with your co-parent can still focus on your child. Discuss how the move will affect custody, scheduling, and your child's ability to remain connected. Increased use of digital communications may help. Quality over quantity will also matter if your child's time with their other parent decreases. Talk to your child about these changes and make space for them to voice their feelings.

Question: "Can it sometimes work to delegate decisions to one co-parent to make in their household?"

Answer: Absolutely. Delegation of responsibility between two homes often works well. Think of how this is done in a work situation: employees have different roles and tasks based on their skill sets. Delegation can be managed by your co-parenting steering committee. For example, you may be good at keeping up with emails from school. Instead of feeling frustrated that you have to remind your co-parent about school events, discuss the advantages of delegating that task to you. Then together identify what your co-parent's jam may be. Maybe they are interested in sports and other after-school programs. You could agree to delegate signing your child up for those events to your co-parent. Appreciate each other for what you bring to the process of managing your child's life.

Question: "What if my co-parent uses my child to pass on information to me?"

Answer: Even if your co-parent does this, you don't have to fall into the same pattern of poor communication. For starters, don't respond or relay anything back through your child. Instead email, text, or call your co-parent directly. Be clear that this is the best way to communicate. You can talk to your child about what is happening, without saying anything negative about the other parent. Ask your child how they feel. For example, you can say, "I noticed your other parent often tells you to remind me about stuff. How is that for you?" Help your child set healthy boundaries. This is also an opportunity to talk to your co-parent about functioning as a united front, which is a topic we will cover more in the next chapter.

Chapter 7

Presenting a United Front

Suppose when you come home after work and open your front door, your home looks totally different. The place is bigger. The furniture's been rearranged. Some rooms have different purposes. Maybe you can't even find the toilet. And—most disconcerting—you have no control over the situation. This is what it's like for your child who has to alternate between two homes that lack consistency.

"But kids are so resilient! They'll manage with two homes." You may have heard this or thought it yourself. However, while research shows that many children are highly resilient (D'Onofrio and Emery 2019), it's unfair to expect a child to simply *be* resilient, to bounce back regardless of the circumstances. Your child is more likely to be resilient if you as co-parents provide structures that support secure attachment. A big part of what gives your child the ability to withstand and adjust to the changes that come with living in a two-home family system is consistency.

In this chapter, we will look at the principle of *consistency*: co-parents build consistent structures in both homes to create reliable and predictable environments. We will explore the role of consistency in developing secure attachment after a separation or divorce. We'll look at how you and your co-parent can implement consistency in your two-home family system, including presenting as a united front; setting up schedules, routines, and other consistent structures; and making the most of transition times. Instead of seeing inconsistencies between your co-parenting styles as a threat to your child's stability, you'll take them as opportunities to improve how you function as a secure co-parenting team. And if your co-parent isn't fully on board with this project, know that you can still provide your child with consistency within your own home.

Consistency and Secure Attachment

Consistency is created when your child can depend on their caregivers to provide predictable home environments. Knowing what to expect and that their needs will be met nurtures confidence, trust, and secure attachment for your child. Think of a tightrope walker who knows that, regardless of how often they fall, they'll be caught by a safety net. As co-parents, you are that net for your child. Walking a tightrope between two homes without a net would feel scary and stressful for your child and potentially cause unhealthy coping patterns that continue into their future.

Let's look at three examples of children experiencing inconsistency in their two homes and how this affects their relationship with one or both co-parents, their sense of secure attachment, and their behavior at home or in school.

Maria, who is six, stopped bed-wetting two years ago, around the time she started sleeping in her own bed. After her parents separated, her mom let Maria sleep with her whenever Maria had a bad dream. Her dad says Maria is too old to sleep in her parent's bed. When Maria started wetting the bed at his house, he blamed her mom. Here, the stress from inconsistent sleeping routines and how her parents respond to Maria's emotions may be causing renewed bed-wetting.

Alex, who uses they/them pronouns, is twelve. Their mother works two jobs and is often home late. She trusts Alex to do their homework and thinks Alex isn't bringing much home. Alex's father works from home and monitors Alex's homework. He complains Alex has too much catch-up work because it wasn't completed at their mother's house. Alex and their father often clash over getting homework done on time. Inconsistent homework routines in these two homes have led to a slip in Alex's grades and overall school performance.

Antonio is seventeen. He stays one week with Dada and one week with Poppa. At Dada's, he has to be home by 11:00 p.m. or he'll lose car privileges. At Poppa's, he has to call in at 9:00 p.m. but can stay out until midnight if Poppa knows where he is. Even if he's late, his car privileges aren't at risk. Antonio gets into battles with Dada and says he'd rather stay at Poppa's. Recently, Dada found a marijuana joint hidden in a book. Antonio is caught between co-parents who haven't provided consistent rules or boundaries. He is struggling emotionally and may be resorting to unhealthy behaviors, including pitting his co-parents against each other. It's a no-win for all involved.

These three kids experience their two-home families as two completely different worlds, where they are expected to behave in different ways to gain love and approval. They're being asked to live two different lives. Of course, consistency does not mean creating two homes that are carbon copies of each other. That's not possible, nor is it expected. However, you can install a safety net and create bridges and areas of overlap to help your kid feel secure within the inherently inconsistent nature of alternating between two houses. Let's look at how you can do this.

Being a United Front

Being a united front offers consistency to your child in the face of differences between co-parents' views and opinions or between how things are done in your two homes. Seeing you and your co-parent as a united team, with a set of shared values and the ability to make decisions together, keeps your child from being confused about how to act in each home. It also minimizes power struggles between you and your child.

When you and your co-parent don't present as a united front, your child will likely let you know. Even if they don't tell you directly how hard it is, you may notice behavioral issues or falling grades in school, as we saw with Alex. Underneath these issues, your child may be screaming for consistency.

If you and your co-parent haven't already done so, agree to present a united front to your child. You can use the following tips to help you be more consistent as you navigate the co-parenting journey together.

Keep Messaging Consistent

Work with your co-parent to come up with similar age-appropriate guidelines for your child to maintain in your two homes. For example, your child's bedtime should be consistent across homes. Your teenager should have consistent rules for staying out late. The boundaries in your respective homes should also be consistent. Discuss with your co-parent the specific expectations you have for your child's behavior and the consequences for not following the boundaries you set. Also discuss how you each will present these messages to your child.

As we saw with Antonio, failing to have consistent messages can cause your child to pit the two of you against each other. If your child tries to use the other parent's rules to bend guidelines at your house, simply acknowledge the difference. Don't try to defend yourself or disparage your co-parent. Then check in with your co-parent when your child isn't around and reassess together. See if you can get on the same page with respect to this difference. And if not, then agree to make it clear to your child that you support each other's decisions. Here are some examples for how to communicate with your child about inconsistencies between homes:

Don't: "I don't care what happens at Dada's house. He's not here."

Do: "Dada and I discussed your curfew again. It's still 11:00 p.m. on weekends in both houses."

Don't: "Your mom is too lax on TV rules. She's not following through on what we decided. Turn it off now!"

Do: "I know you want to watch more TV. Your mom and I have different rules on this, and it can be confusing. Here you have half an hour of TV. So let's get those pajamas on now."

Never Play Tug-of-War with Your Kids

Have two people ever pulled your arms in opposite directions? It feels like you're being split in half! That's what happens when inconsistency or lack of unity puts your child in the middle. This can take various forms, including using your child to find out information about the other parent and asking them to relay info or items to the other parent. Your child is not your spy or messenger. Don't ask them to choose between you and their other parent.

Don't: "Would you prefer to go with Mom to Michigan or stay here with me?"

Do: "Your mom and I will discuss holiday plans and let you know as soon as we know."

Don't: "You went ice-skating, how fun! Was your dad's girlfriend there?"

Do: "You went ice-skating, how fun!"

Never Throw Each Other Under the Bus

Saying negative or judgmental things about your co-parent confuses and hurts your child. It can even lower your child's self-esteem. Your child identifies with both of you, and their self-esteem draws from that identity. When you say something negative about your co-parent, your child may think you're also speaking about them. For example, if you say, "Your dad never does anything right," your child may think, *I love Dad, and he's part of me, so this must mean I can't do anything right.* They may feel confused about loving the other parent and worry, *What does it mean about me if I love this bad person?* And their self-esteem takes a hit. Even if you hear that your child's other parent said negative things about you, don't engage in this kind of warfare using your child as the bullet. Your child will end up more shattered and destroyed than your ex.

Don't: "Your dad never shows up."

Do: "I sent your dad the invite to your violin recital."

Don't: "You know how to make me mad, just like your mom does."

Do: "I'm feeling angry right now."

Don't: "What your dad is telling you is wrong. Don't listen to him!"

Do: "Your dad and I sometimes disagree. That's okay. We both love and care about you. This is a chance to learn about different views. When you're older, you can form your own opinion about this."

Use the following exercise with your co-parent to assess how well you present a united front for your child and what you can do to improve.

Are We United?

You can do this exercise at a steering committee meeting (see chapter 6) or other routine check-in time with your co-parent. Ask each other the following questions:

- *In what ways did we operate as a united front when we were still together?*

- *How are we operating as a united front now?*

- *In what situations do we succeed at presenting a united front?*

- *In what situations do we need to be more united?*

- *What specifically can each of us do to achieve a more united front?*

- *How can we help each other become more united?*

Allow your responses to guide you in presenting a more united front to your child.

While discussing how you and your co-parent can be more united, you may consider some specifics related to scheduling, routines, and other structures in your respective homes. A consistent schedule will help your child feel comfortable and at home in both of their houses.

Scheduling

As co-parents, you can help your child handle the complications of living in two homes by setting up and maintaining a schedule for when your child will be in each home. This schedule creates a foundation your child can rely on. Your child feels, for example, *I can relax knowing I'll see Mom on Mondays and Tuesdays.* In addition to the days in each home, your schedule should include regular activities, such as sports and art classes. It can also incorporate special events and occasions, such as birthdays, holidays, and vacations. Post the schedule in a prominent place in each house so everyone can refer to it.

You may need to follow input from a court, or you may be able to create this schedule independently. Here are some examples of schedules that can work.

- One week with you and the next week with your co-parent

- Two days with you, then two with your co-parent

- Two days with you, then two with your co-parent, then alternate weekends

- Three days with you, four days with your co-parent, then four with you, followed by three with your co-parent

Although these schedules are fifty-fifty, you and your co-parent may choose another arrangement, such as sixty-forty, if it better suits your child's needs. You may also choose the bird-nesting approach, whereby your child and all their belongings stay in the same house, and the parents alternate. Depending on your job or how far apart you live, a schedule that gives you quality time—rather than more time—with your child may be best.

While some kids adjust easily to switching between homes, others struggle. Generally, younger children need more consistent and frequent contact with both parents to develop secure attachment, while older children may want more say in their schedule and don't mind longer times apart from one parent. A toddler may benefit from switching homes every two days, while a teen whose school is closer to one co-parent's home may request more time there. Consistency could entail showing up for your child even when it's not your parenting time.

Setting up a consistent schedule doesn't mean being rigid. While constant changes can be disruptive, occasional shifts are to be expected. Flexibility is key for working as a united team. For example, if your co-parent breaks a leg and requires surgery, discuss what this will mean for your schedule, and let your child know about any necessary adjustments, so they're prepared.

It may take a bit of trial and error to find the plan that best meets the needs of your family, and your schedule will likely evolve over time. Holidays and other special events can present scheduling challenges. As you plan ahead, think about how you want your kid to feel and how they will remember these moments with you. What new holiday traditions do you want to create? For example, your child could have Thanksgiving with one co-parent and Rosh Hashanah with the other. You can alternate years. Or your child could spend a few hours on Christmas morning with both co-parents, provided you can do this without tension. What's important is that your child doesn't feel they must split themselves between the two of you to make you happy. Finally, your child's birthday is their special day. Some parents find neutral ground to host a party. Or you could take turns hosting on alternate years. I don't recommend two parties, because it can create competition that puts your child in the middle.

Routines and Other Structures

Routines and structures can provide consistency both between and within your homes. Whereas *routines* are sets of activities that are repeated on a regular basis, *structures* are ways to organize life so it runs smoothly in your home. What your child does each night before going to sleep is their bedtime routine; the time they go to bed and which bed they sleep in are structures. You and your co-parent can create routines and structures that are similar across your homes. They don't need to be identical, just similar enough for your child to get the same message and know what to expect. At the same time, following routines consistently within your own home— regardless of whether they're in place elsewhere—will give your child a sense of security.

The first step in achieving consistency across your homes is to determine where you already are consistent and where you're not. The following exercise could help you work toward greater consistency between your two homes.

Two Homes, One Life

Sit down with your co-parent and make a list of the routines and structures in both your homes. Here is a list to consider. Feel free to expand on it (such as listing different chores). Routines will change as your child's needs change.

- childcare

- sleeping arrangements

- bedtime routines

- mealtimes

- homework

- chores

- boundaries

- consequences for behavior

- screen time, TV, social media, phones

- curfews

Discuss how you handle each of these things in your respective homes. You can include relevant experiences from prior to your separation. Focus on identifying inconsistencies.

Then discuss how you can eliminate inconsistencies that may be affecting your child. Identify the specific changes each of you will make in your homes to achieve this. For example, suppose that before your separation, your child had TV time for half an hour before bedtime. Maintaining that structure in both your homes now will help your child know what to expect. If one of you prefers alternating TV time with reading time, discuss whether you both want to do this to maintain consistency. If you can't find a middle ground, discuss how to talk with your child about differences between homes. In general, the more consistent you can be, the better.

Let's look more closely at four structures or routines that come up frequently as bones of contention between co-parents: sleeping arrangements, bedtime routines, mealtimes, and homework.

Sleeping Arrangements

Now that your child has two homes, they also have two bedrooms. Creating consistent sleeping arrangements can help your infant or young child feel comfortable and ease the discomfort of a new environment. Some structures to consider as you strive for greater consistency:

- co-sleeping or not

- bed type (for example, crib or bed)

- sleepwear and bedding

- toys or other comfort items

For an older child, having a say in how each of their rooms is decorated gives them a sense of choice and ownership in each home.

Co-parents who do the "Two Homes, One Life" exercise may find it relatively easy to coordinate consistency with things such as bed type. But what if they disagree on their values related to sleep arrangements? Earlier in this chapter, I described Maria, who was bed-wetting at her father's house. Even though her parents had conflicting philosophies about sleeping arrangements, they were able to come to an agreement. Here's how.

First, Maria's parents found common ground: they both acknowledged Maria was struggling, and their priority was to address her needs. Then they agreed that because she'd slept well in her own bed before, she should continue to do that. Aware that some children regress after a separation, they agreed Maria needed extra soothing. However, they decided to soothe her while she was in her own bed. This solution satisfied both the father, who wanted Maria to sleep in her own bed, and the mother, who wanted Maria to be comforted. With this structure in place, Maria's bed-wetting abated, and she was back to sleeping through the night.

Bedtime Routines

Even with consistent sleeping arrangements, sleep disturbances are common among children with two homes. If you have a baby, you may notice more fussiness or frequent waking. If you have a toddler or school-age child, you may notice more nightmares or anxieties. Teens may develop unhealthy sleep habits or sleep disorders. You can guard against these issues by creating routines for lights-out and wake-up times. Routines such as the following have been shown to have a positive impact on language development, literacy, and secure attachment (Mindell and Williamson 2018):

- Bedtime snack, such as a warm drink

- Toothbrushing and other hygiene routines

- Gratitude moments, including mindfulness practices or prayers

- Affirmations and reminders of how much they are loved

- Goodnight kisses or hugs

- Reading or story time; songs

- Sharing both positive and challenging moments from the day

You can also come up with similar routines for waking up in the morning.

Mealtimes

Mealtimes may be triggering after a separation if your child is used to having dinner with both parents on a regular basis. However, when managed with consistency, mealtimes can have a positive impact on your child's emotional well-being, health, and literacy and language development (Barton et al. 2019). For this reason, you want to make mealtimes a daily anchor within the busyness and chaos of the day. Here are some ways to create consistency around meals:

- Eat at the same time you did before the separation.

- Talk to your child about their day and their interests.

- Let your child claim and maintain their seat at the table.

- Give your child a job to do at every meal, such as setting or clearing the table or folding napkins.

Some co-parents like to maintain a shared family meal routine. If you feel you can do this in a tension-free way, discuss setting a consistent day and time for a family meal with your child.

Homework

Having a homework routine that is similar in both homes can minimize parent-child conflicts and help them stay on track with their studies. Remember Alex, who was struggling with different homework routines in their two homes? Here's how the conversation between their co-parents, Chris and Jo, went when they did the "Two Homes, One Life" exercise:

Chris: Alex is fighting with me every day about homework. Do you have a regular homework time at your house?

Jo: Not really. I didn't think it was an issue.

Chris: If we could find a consistent routine, I don't think it would be an issue, and I wouldn't have to push so hard.

Jo: Got it.

Chris: I always have Alex do homework before hanging out with friends.

Jo: That makes sense. I make sure there's a snack available when Alex gets home. That could be part of the homework routine.

Chris:	Good idea. And a consistent place to study. Here, Alex likes the kitchen table.
Jo:	That would work here too.
Chris:	I always make it clear I'm available for questions.
Jo:	I am, too, if I'm not too busy. But most days, I don't get home from work until later. I could ask at dinner time if they have any questions.
Chris:	Sounds good. Thanks for working this out with me. I hope this will help Alex.

In this scenario, the co-parents work together to create a consistent routine across their homes. Because the overall routine is consistent, we can assume Alex will be okay with some variation—in this case, how available each parent is for assistance. These co-parents might also ask Alex to develop a homework chart listing assignments and study goals that can be applied across homes.

Being creative and designing routines and structures that emphasize your child's strengths supports them in areas where they struggle. One reality of two-home family life is transitions. While there is no question that transitions can be hard, let's look at ways to minimize the stress.

Good Goodbyes and Better Hellos

Transitions are moments of separation and reunion. They happen every morning when you drop your child off at school and every afternoon when you pick them up. You might not think of these as transitions, but transitions occur when your child wakes up in the morning and when they go to sleep at night. Going to a new school or moving to a new home are major transitions. For a kid living in two homes, transitions occur each time they leave one home and arrive at the other. A transition can be as small as getting on or off the phone with their parent.

Why are transitions so important? As mentioned in chapter 1, Mary Ainsworth based her seminal research on attachment theory on what happens to children when they separate from and then are reunited with a primary caregiver. From that and subsequent studies, we know most children feel some level of distress or discomfort from separations. However, a child with secure attachment can manage separations with more ease and is able to reengage quickly with their parent. A child with ambivalent attachment may show more extreme signs of distress or be clingy during separations and resist reconnections with a parent. They're not easily soothed when reunited. A child with avoidant attachment may not show obvious signs of distress but does experience it internally. They may ignore their parent when reunited.

Sometimes co-parents misconstrue their child's resistance and tears at transition moments as issues with the other parent. But if your child is able to adjust after that moment, then it's more likely the transition itself is stressful, not the other home. You can help your child by making transitions free of tension and conflict, maintaining consistent structures on transition days, and making sure your child never feels they have to choose between the two of you or take care of your feelings. The following sections include some tips and guidelines for handling transitions with consistency.

The Anticipation

Children need time to prepare emotionally and mentally for transitions. Letting your child know what to expect ahead of time can help them prepare for an upcoming transition. When they know what to expect, they'll feel more in control. My child learned the days of the week because of the predictable structure of her days with me and days with her dad. She felt empowered by her own knowledge. Here are a few tips to ease the anticipation of a separation.

Helpful reminders. Let your child know the who, what, where, and when of each transition. The day before, remind your child they will be going to their other parent's home the next day. The morning of the transition, remind them again.

Visual cues. Have your child's schedule visibly accessible. This can be a calendar or other visual representation. You can hang it in their room or on the fridge. Have them write in or color in the days at each home. Teens may prefer to have their calendar on their devices.

Validate and reassure. Validate that transitions and saying goodbye are hard and stressful. Empathize with your child's feelings and remind them they can do it. "It's okay to feel sad about leaving and be happy to see your other parent, even if that's sometimes confusing." Remind your child how much you love them and how much their other parent loves them, and that you're happy they get to spend time with you both. You can talk about what they enjoy at both homes.

The Day Of

On transition days stick to your daily routines. The more consistency and predictability on transition days, the better. Consider keeping some of your child's activities to a minimum, so you can have more quality time. You want their transition days to be full of connection and laughter. Even if you're typically rushing out the door to school, you can incorporate a few minutes of connection time before the day starts. A morning snuggle, a playful roughhouse tumble, breakfast together, or reading a short book can go a long way on these days.

Connection time is important for kids of all ages, including teens. It can be easy for busy teens to skip over time with you, as they focus on time with friends, but that doesn't make it less important. For younger kids, plan playdates, social activities, and adventures on other days. Here are a few tips for a smooth transition day.

Time and location. Choose a time of day that suits your child's rhythms (for example, morning rather than late in the day) and a neutral location (school or library). Some kids do better with drop-offs than pick-ups. Keep your goodbyes short and sweet.

Keep it child-focused. Especially if your child is upset, stay present with their feelings. Avoid bringing in your own or your co-parent's feelings, so your child doesn't feel they're causing you or your co-parent pain or feel they have to take care of either parent. For example, instead of "Your mom will be frustrated if you are late," try "I know it's hard to leave. Let's be on time."

You do the waiting. Being a little early to pick up your child, so they don't have to wait for you, will reduce the anxiety that can build up during transitions. Bring something to do in the car or wherever you're waiting, so you don't feel like you're wasting time.

Transitional objects. Some kids like to keep an object with them that reminds them of their parent. Examples include pictures, toys, and a note in their lunch box. My daughter has a picture of her with each of us in her respective rooms. She and I have matching rings. The pencil case she uses every day at school is special because she made it with her dad.

Their things. Allow your child to take what they want to their other home. Let them wear what they want to wear. There's nothing that screams "visitor" more than arriving and departing with a suitcase. They should have what they need at both homes and feel that their stuff is always welcome there.

The following exercise is one of my favorites to do while on your way to dropping your child off.

The Five Senses Mindfulness Game

This game can be played in a car, on the bus, while walking, or in whatever form of transportation you use. Take turns with your child and ask the following questions:

What are you seeing? What are you smelling? What are you touching? What are you tasting? What are you hearing?

Each of these questions can become a conversation. The age of your child will also determine how detailed you want to get. Here's an example.

You: "What are you seeing?"

Your child: "Leaves on the tree."

You: "And what color are those leaves?"

Your child: "Green."

You: "Dark or light green?"

And so on.

This five-senses exercise is a mindfulness moment that helps ground your child in the present, which can reduce their anxiety and foster connection with you.

Transition Rituals

A *ritual* is a type of routine that implies a greater sense of meaning and purpose. You can develop rituals to help you bridge the divide during separations and create greater consistency and security for your child. Transition rituals can infuse the routine of separating and reuniting with expressions of love and security.

Every time I drop Ellie off, we say "I love you!" I give her a kiss and look into her eyes as I remind her of exactly when I will see her again. For example, "I'll pick you up from school on Thursday." Then, as she's walking toward her school or toward her other house, we blow each other a kiss.

This has been our simple ritual since she was six. She is now eleven, and we basically do the same thing every time.

Children are sensitive to our feelings. Sometimes co-parents say "I'll miss you" when their child goes to the other parent's house. In fact, those words can lead your child to feel they make you sad when they leave. Instead, consider saying something like "I love you so much. I'll be thinking about you. And I'm excited to see you this weekend." Of course, if your child says it first, you can respond accordingly: "I'll miss you too, because I love you so much. I'll see you this weekend." If they say they miss their other parent, you might say, "Of course, you miss your dad, because you love him!"

The following exercise will help you create some rituals to share with your child. Depending on their age, they may even take the lead in coming up with a goodbye or hello ritual.

Goodbye and Hello Moments

Create a goodbye ritual. This marks your moment of separation. It could include an "I love you" exchange, your own special hug or kiss, or pretty much anything unique to your relationship.

Then create a hello ritual. This marks the moment of reconnection after your separation. It's your way to say "Welcome home" as your child enters into their space with you.

Practice these rituals each and every time you and your child separate and reunite. Let the rituals evolve over time, if that feels right, so they are always alive and vibrant for you and your child.

Even if your child's emotions run high, the use of routines and rituals can help you be the rock they come home to that is consistent and present. In the next chapter, we'll look at how you can use inner consistency in the form of emotional presence and connection to create a more secure attachment for your child.

● ● Now What? ● ●

Question: "I have a hard time showing up as a united front at our kid's games, especially when my co-parent makes annoying comments."

Answer: Even if you're committed to presenting a united front, you may not always be mentally and emotionally in that place. I suggest a "fake it till you make it" approach. Even if you find your co-parent annoying, make the extra effort to be cordial or friendly. If a game lands on your parenting day, you and your co-parent can both go. You can sit apart. If you're truly too uncomfortable to be in the same space without tension, discuss ways to show up for your child at different times. For example, you might alternate attendance at games.

Question: "My sixteen-year-old wants to get a job so he can save for a car. I said okay, but then realized I hadn't discussed it with my co-parent. How do I manage that?"

Answer: Discussions about your child's interests will occur naturally in your household—sometimes before your co-parent can get involved. However, you can bring this to your steering committee meeting (see chapter 6) after the fact. Let your co-parent know your son wants to find a job and that you agreed it was a good opportunity. In addition, let your son know you need to talk to their other parent before he takes any action. If it turns out your co-parent has different ideas, you'll need to discuss how best to present a united front. Your son is old enough to understand that you may have different values related to money as well as different ideas about getting to and from the job and how to balance the job and homework.

Question: "My co-parent has a bigger house, and our kids have their own rooms there, which isn't possible in my tiny apartment. Is that harmful?"

Answer: No. What's important is that your kids feel they have a sense of belonging in both homes. Talk about the differences openly, without shame or judgment. That will help them learn about and navigate the discrepancies in income and resources that characterize our society, along with the normal ups and downs of childhood. Ultimately, as a co-parent, your own home is the only place you have control over. But you can make it a sanctuary—a place your kids can walk in the door, drop their school bags, shed their outdoor gear, and find consistent structures that feel safe, familiar, and reliable.

Chapter 8

Creating Secure Kids

Thus far, we have focused on how you, as co-parents, can establish a solid foundation for your co-parenting triangle. But really the focal point of your triangle—and the main character in your new family story—is your kid. So let's shine our spotlight toward the top of the triangle and look at how you can best help them understand their thoughts and feelings about your separation.

From the moment you tell your child about your breakup, they're likely to experience a kaleidoscope of emotions and thoughts. Even if they had secure attachment before, they are suddenly faced with the inconsistencies that arise from going between homes. They may see one parent more than the other. The quality of the relationship they have with one or both parents may shift. Also, they have just learned the shocking reality that parents don't always stay together and love doesn't always last. All of this can cause fear and grief and anger, and even long-lasting trauma, if left unprocessed.

In chapter 2, we discussed the various emotions you may cycle through as a co-parent, especially as a new co-parent. Your child is vulnerable to a similar spectrum of emotions when they experience the loss of their family unit as they knew it, and they need you to help them process those emotions. By *process*, I mean understand, accept, and regulate their emotions.

In this chapter, we will focus on the principle of *connection*: co-parents stay present and mindful with their child to help them process their emotions and to build secure attachment. We will explore how you can create this connection by being present with your child. We will also discuss how to tune into your child's emotions and their associated sensations, so you can help them process their grief, thus minimizing trauma and maximizing security in your home.

Your Child's Attachment Style

In chapter 1, you observed your child to get a sense of their attachment style. If you haven't already been doing so regularly, you may want to revisit that observation process now. Because your child's attachment style is based on their relationship with their parents, let's explore how your presence with your child can foster secure attachment. Here is one family's story. See if you can identify some of the behaviors we discussed in chapter 1.

- *Kia and Zephyr*

  Kia and Zephyr are a nine-year-old sister and five-year-old brother. Their parents separated two years ago and share parenting time equally. Dad is still mourning the end of the relationship and often cries or gets angry about it. Mom, who initiated the separation, has moved on to a new relationship. Kia started having outbursts after the family house, where Dad had been living, was sold. She told her mom she hated her life and wouldn't leave on moving day. When her mom suggested she'd feel better when she saw Dad's great new home, she responded by slamming the door and kicking it.

  Zephyr, on the other hand, appears easygoing and unemotional. When he first heard about his parents' separation, he looked stunned for a moment and then walked off to his room to play with his toys. After that, he didn't engage whenever Dad tried to talk to him about what was happening. Following the sale of the house, Zephyr had stomachaches off and on for a year. The doctor found nothing physically wrong, so Mom thought he was just trying to get attention and told him to stop pretending, because he'll "be fine." She thought it was amusing when she overheard him telling a friend that his parents had to live in two homes because they had too much stuff for one home.

These siblings are experiencing similar situations but reacting with different attachment styles. Kia's ambivalent attachment shows up in her emotional outbursts. Although anger is a normal part of grieving a loss, she expresses it in an exaggerated way because she doesn't feel heard by her parents. Her father's clinging to his former relationship with Kia's mom and his inability to regulate his emotions—signs of his ambivalent attachment—exacerbate Kia's insecurity. Losing their house, which felt like her last hope for the family getting back together, further triggers Kia's fears and insecurity. With her tantrums, Kia is screaming "I'm not okay. I need you!"

Zephyr's avoidant attachment leads him to shut down and self-soothe in his room. Like Kia, he feels the loss of their old home, but he displays his distress through the avoidant tendency of withdrawing. His mother's own avoidant tendencies have led her to completely discount what he is feeling. Even though Zephyr may seem fine to his parents and his doctor, his chronic stomachaches are his body's way of telling the world he's actually not fine.

In general, a child with secure or ambivalent attachment can process their grief or distress faster than a child with avoidant attachment because they are expressing their emotions. However, the key factor is how their parents respond to their child's distress. Kia and Zephyr's co-parents may be well-meaning, but they are missing their kids' signals of distress. Each child's reactions reflect the quality of their attachment with their parents. For this reason, one starting point for these parents is to increase awareness of their own attachment styles. This doesn't mean you have to fundamentally change your style before you can create security for your child.

However, you do need to recognize that how you each respond to your child will have an impact on their attachment security.

You may notice that your child is clingy and expressive with you and seems more shut down with their other parent. Or vice versa. That's because your child's attachment style can reflect that of one or both parents. Moreover, just as with adults, a child's attachment style can fluctuate, depending on current crises. Specific situations (such as the loss of a parent) and their age, personality, and birth order are all potential factors. Thus, it isn't surprising for two siblings to display different attachment styles following their parents' breakup.

Regardless of your own attachment style, you can identify your child's signals of distress and respond in helpful ways. If your child was securely attached prior to your breakup, you can work to keep them feeling secure. If they already had insecure attachment patterns, you can work to adjust that now. The primary way to do so is to be present and engaged with your child. Your role in your child's security is paramount. The presence of an attachment figure who is attuned to their emotional well-being is one of the most important factors in your child's ability to weather a separation. Having positive relationships with both parents further supports their security and ability to be resilient.

Being Present with Your Child

As a co-parent, seeing your child in emotional pain related to your breakup can cause so much guilt and shame and pain in you that you find it hard to be present with your child. In addition to the realities of your busy life, the force of your own emotions can make it hard to be there for your child. Their emotions can trigger your own past traumas. I get it: it's not easy to remain present when emotions are running high!

No matter how much you might like to wave a magic wand to take away your child's pain, you can't do that. However, if you retain your calm and stay present and empathetic with your child, they can get through these experiences without lasting trauma. It is not enough to spend time in the same physical space as your child; you must also be fully engaged and aware. The recipe for connection is being available and attuned during times of distress as well as joy. Connection is fundamental to feeling secure.

Children are deeply tuned in to their parents. If your child senses their emotions are causing stress or upsetting you, they may find ways to turn that feeling off or "to be strong." They don't want to feel like they are hurting you. They may even try to console *you*, flipping the roles and becoming miniparents or confidants to their adult parent. These behaviors lead to insecure attachment patterns of avoidance and caretaking as a means to maintain safety, connection, and lovability. In essence, your child is losing not only their family unit but also their childhood. The way to avoid this is to connect with your child and offer loving and unconditional support. You will then build the trust they need to feel safe and secure.

It can be hard to stay present with an angry child who is yelling or throwing things. Your whole body may feel like screaming back or calling it quits. However, instead of trying to reprimand them, if you bring empathy and show that you understand the emotions and needs your child is trying to communicate through their behaviors, the outburst will subside. Your presence is saying "I hear you. I see you. I get you." And you can reinforce that verbally as well. When your child feels seen and valued in this way, they will develop a basis of self-confidence from which to explore and find solutions to any problems that arise.

Moments of connection can happen spontaneously throughout the day, but creating intentional connection time with your child helps them feel seen and secure and ensures that quality time doesn't get lost in the shuffle. I recommend incorporating this time into your existing routines. If at any point you notice your stress and emotions becoming overwhelming and making it hard to be present with your child, consider talking with a therapist, spiritual counselor, or coach.

Connection Time

Create a special connection time to engage with your child every day. Turn off your phone and put other distractions aside, so you can spend quality time with your child. It doesn't have to be a long time; ten to fifteen minutes per day can make a world of difference.

Here are some activities you can do during your connection time:

- **Play.** Your child can use toys, dolls, blocks, and other things to create stories and characters.

- **Act it out.** Your child can make up a story and give you a character to act out.

- **Do art.** Draw, paint, use clay, or craft together.

- **Use media.** Ask your child to share their favorite songs or play DJ for you. Play a video game with them. Watch and talk about their favorite TV show.

- **Play games.** Playing a card or board game can create a safe place to talk or just be together.

- **Cook.** Bake cookies, make lemonade, or cook your kid's favorite meal or snack together.

- **Tell or write a story.** You and your child can make up a story together. Let them create the characters and story line, then follow along.

- **Read together.** Allow your child to choose the book. They may choose a book they've read many times before.

- **Take a walk or hike.** Choose a location your child enjoys with a path wide enough for you to walk side by side.

- **Roughhouse.** Choose a safe space, such as a bed, and play-wrestle, tickle, and laugh.

- **Use humor.** Joke around and be silly with your kid.

> - **Positive touch.** Provide nurturing touch throughout your child's day; offer hugs, kisses, back rubs, snuggles, cuddles. All physical touch must be consensual.
>
> The activities you do together will change as your child grows. Let your child take the lead in choosing activities. Don't take over an activity or unnecessarily ask questions: just observe, stay curious, and have fun.

During connection time, you will learn a lot about what your child thinks and feels, and your child will feel free to release emotions when they want to. Let's look more specifically at how to increase attunement to your child's emotions.

Tuning in to Your Child's Emotions

Being attuned to a child's emotions is important for all parents, at all times. But if you've recently gone through a separation, being mindful and attuned may carry extra challenges. For example, your previously independent child may now be more clingy at drop-offs, become anxious before going to bed, be withdrawn, or get into trouble at school. These are ways of expressing their need to be seen and reassured by you.

A child's ability to regulate their emotions develops at a different stage than their attachment style does and involves different parts of the brain. Attachment develops in the first eighteen months of life (Bowlby 1988) and is centered in the downstairs brain—specifically, the right hemisphere of your child's brain and their limbic and autonomic nervous systems (Schore 2001). In contrast, the prefrontal cortex, which allows for the ability to understand and regulate emotions, typically isn't fully developed until approximately age twenty-five (Arain et al. 2013).

What does this mean for you as a parent? As you build connection with your child, you also help them become aware of and learn to regulate their emotions. For example, when you smile lovingly into your baby's eyes, they smile back and feel soothed. However, if you get overwhelmed or stressed when your baby cries, they will become more agitated. Your child will continue to take cues from you as they grow.

The stresses associated with a separation or divorce accentuate your child's needs for emotional support. Be alert to any distress signals they may be shooting your way (such as tantrums, refusing to eat, power struggles, apathy, changes in behavior or academic performance, and physical pains). When your child is in the throes of an emotion, their nervous system is running on high. First make sure your own nervous system is calm. Then you can connect and hold space for their emotions, so their nervous system starts to move toward neutral again. Through your consistent connection, they will increase their ability to self-regulate.

In the next sections, we will look at two emotional reactions your child may have following a breakup: trauma and grief. I single out these two because they are especially common. Then I will introduce you to some tools you can use not only with trauma and grief but with all the emotions your child may be experiencing.

Trauma

Trauma happens when someone experiences an event that is frightening, stressful, or intense and that occurs suddenly, typically with little or no explanation or comfort. Separation or divorce can be traumatic for a child, especially if they are left to try to understand the changes and their feelings on their own. A child with secure attachment can likely process the feelings associated with this situation and adjust. That is not the case, however, for a child who is continually a witness to their parents' conflict, is put in the middle of their parents' decisions, or feels they have to take sides. Such a child is more likely to develop insecurity or fear of abandonment, feel they are at fault, or hold on to the fantasy of their parents reuniting well past the separation and into adulthood.

Shutting down (as with Zephyr) and physical aggression toward others (as with Kia) or oneself are among the signs that a child has trauma that needs to be processed. You can help your child move out of potential trauma by being present and connected with them and, if necessary, seeking consultation with a therapist.

Grief

Grief is the process an individual goes through in response to a loss. Separation and divorce are losses for everyone involved. For your child, it is the loss of the only home and family unit they knew—of stability, routines, and seeing both parents every day. Grief can be an aspect of trauma, but grief does not need to turn into full-blown trauma. A child who has a present caregiver can generally process their grief in a healthy way.

It can be helpful to become familiar with the five basic stages of grief: denial, anger, bargaining, depression, and acceptance (Kübler-Ross and Kessler 2005). Every child cycles through these stages in their own way and not necessarily in order. All these stages are important parts of the healing journey. There is no right or wrong way to experience grief, nor is there a set time frame. Grief has both emotional and physical manifestations. Some—such as stomachaches, headaches, sleep disturbances, academic issues—can occur at any stage.

Just as you observed your child to get a sense of their attachment style, you can notice emotions, thoughts, and behaviors that suggest which, if any, stage of grief your child may be experiencing. The goal is not to try to stop or "fix" their feelings but rather to give your child the support, understanding, and compassion they need.

Let's look at each of the five stages of grief.

DENIAL

A child in the denial stage isn't able to take in and absorb that their parents' breakup has happened. You may notice your child do the following at home or in school:

- Not tell others about your breakup or separation

- Make up false reasons for the breakup

- Act confused, change the subject, deny feelings

- Draw pictures or talk of their family as still intact

Your child may be numb or in shock. It may feel too scary to take in reality. In an effort to cope with their pain, they may make up stories or tell themselves, *This can't be real!* or *This won't last.*

ANGER

A child in the anger stage starts to take in the fact of what has happened. Anger can become an avenue to express their feelings about their loss. They may display frustration, aggression, disappointment, or anxiety outwardly, or they may direct it inwardly.

You may notice your child do the following at home or in school:

- Have emotional outbursts and temper tantrums

- Be defiant; test limits

- Display silent hostility

- Stomp around, bite, kick, yell

Your child may feel helpless, sad, unseen, or disempowered. They may blame one or both parents or themselves: "I hate you," "This isn't fair," "If I were different, maybe my parents would still be together," or "This is my fault."

BARGAINING

A child in the bargaining stage feels they can and need to fix the situation, to get back what they lost. Guilt and wishful thinking show up as they try to gain some level of control and get things back to normal, so they feel safe again.

You may notice your child do the following at home or in school:

- Become the "perfect child" or the "problem child"

- Try to get both parents in the same place, such as by creating an emergency so both parents have to be at the hospital together

- Idealize an absent parent

- Focus on the needs of their parents at the expense of their own needs

Your child may be thinking, *If I'm sick, my parents might get back together* or *If I'm super good, my parents might reunite* or *If only I had cleaned my room more, my parents wouldn't have fought.*

DEPRESSION

A child in the depression stages has realized bargaining won't bring their parents back together. Nothing they can do will fix the situation. They may feel sad, lonely, lethargic, helpless, or overwhelmed.

You may notice your child do the following at home or in school:

- Cry, be tearful, get upset easily

- Withdraw from social situations or activities they previously enjoyed

- Lack energy, have difficulty focusing

- Self-harm or have suicidal thoughts

Depression can feel like a heavy cloud overshadowing everything and shutting down their emotional system. They may feel like running away. They may think, *Why go on? What's the point?* or *I hate my life! I wish I'd never been born.*

ACCEPTANCE

A child in the acceptance stage has come to terms with their parents' breakup. They can acknowledge the loss and adapt to the changes. They feel calm and emotionally stable.

You may notice your child do the following at home or in school:

- Adjust to the new norms

- Be more cooperative and emotionally balanced

- Handle transitions and changes with more ease

- Find joy in social activities and in school

If they have moved away from secure attachment, they may regain it. They may think, *I'm okay. This isn't ideal, but it's what is happening* or *I understand that living in two homes is final.*

Even if you didn't grow up in a family that talked much about feelings, you can change that pattern by helping your child build their vocabulary of feelings. Table 2 lists twenty common feelings your child may be experiencing.

Table 2. Common Feelings

Afraid	Lonely	Happy
Disappointed	Worried	Confused
Loved	Sad	Disgusted/ grossed out
Embarrassed	Frustrated	Unloved
Excited	Guilty	Peaceful
Angry	Ignored	Ashamed
Out of control	Empathetic	Annoyed

Now that you know about the stages of grief and various emotions your child may be feeling, here is an exercise you can do with them.

Let's Talk About Feelings

Share the list of emotions in table 2 with your child, and do any or all of the following.

- Ask your child if and how often they have each of these feelings. You can use a rating system of 1 to 5, where 1 is never and 5 is very often.

- Ask your child to describe a specific time they had each of the feelings they rated 5. When was it? What led to the feeling?

- Discuss any feelings your child is unfamiliar with. Share your own experience of those feelings.

- You may want to use pictures, stories, books, or media to generate topics for discussion.

Feel free to add as many emotion words to table 2 as you (or your child!) can think of. If your child is young, you can simplify the words. Either way, this exercise can be adapted for children of all ages.

Expanding your child's *emotional literacy*—their awareness and recognition of their own feelings and how to manage them—is a first step in helping them regulate their emotions. Now let's explore some tools for connecting with your child to help them process their emotions.

Tools for Your Connection Toolbelt

A child's expression of emotionality is normal and healthy. Children of all ages have big expressions of emotion, so don't be worried. If anything, your child *not* expressing emotions should be cause for concern. Your child needs to cycle through their emotions associated with your breakup as well as any other emotions they have. In the case of grief, they need to express their anger or sadness or disappointment, so they don't get stuck in that stage.

Try the following tools for emotional connection. Some will resonate better with your child than others.

Talk About It

Children follow our lead, so talk openly and in a neutral tone with your child about all their feelings and fantasies. Ask open-ended questions. Discuss their fears. When talking about your breakup, you can use books, movies, or TV shows to start the conversation and normalize their feelings. You can say, "You're not alone." "It's normal."

Simply Be with Your Child

Sometimes a child doesn't need any words. The pressure to talk can cause your child to clam up, even if you're being curious and caring. In that case, it's enough to know their parent is present and can accept their emotional cyclone, without trying to fix or shut them down. Even when your child is crying or yelling, just be with them, calmly and quietly witnessing, holding them, or sitting close by.

Observe Without Judgment

When you notice your child behaving in a certain way, instead of trying to fix or punish a behavior, use empathy and compassion. Ask yourself: *What is my child experiencing? What in their environment may be stressful or cause discomfort? What might they need? What do I need to remain calm in this situation?*

Leave the Door Open

If your child isn't ready to talk to you in the moment about what they are feeling, let them know you will be available when they are ready:

- "It's okay if you don't want to talk now. I'm here for you any time you're ready."

- "Even though you'll be at your other home, I'm here for you. You can call if you want to say hi."

- "I'm glad you shared your disappointment. Let's figure this out together."

- "I love you always and no matter what. My love doesn't change when you're sad, angry, happy, or struggling."

The key is to let them know that you're always available to hear them.

Seize the Moment

You never know when your child will be ready to open up. But when they do want to talk, seize the moment and without any expectations of how long the moment will last.

Listen with Active Curiosity

Bring your curiosity as you observe, and actively listen to your child. In contrast with *passive* listening (observing without judgment), *active* listening includes engagement. Engage with their stories. Encourage them to speak about their feelings. Ask about their experiences:

- "How was that for you?"

- "I wonder what's making you feel this way?"

- "I've noticed you've been really quiet today. What's going on?"

- "Let's figure this out together. What do you need?"

- "Tell me more."

Using a soft and compassionate tone can go a long way.

Reflect Their Feelings

Your child may not always know what they're feeling. You can help them identify those feelings by reflecting back what you observe and checking whether it resonates with them. For a younger child, it can be helpful to get down to eye level as you talk. For teens, stay casual and let them lead. Here are some examples:

- "You're *really* mad right now."

- "You're scared because Mom isn't here to tuck you in tonight. Is that right?"

- "Yeah, you're disappointed. I get it. You wanted to go on that trip, and now you can't."

- "It sounds like going to a new school with new friends is harder than you thought it would be."

- "You look worried about something."

- "It makes sense that you're both sad and angry. Sometimes we can feel two things at the same time, without knowing why."

- "You look so happy! I'm glad we get to do this together!"

Notice that these validations reflect positive as well as negative feelings.

Validate Their Feelings

When you can acknowledge and accept your child's feelings and experiences—without trying to fix or change them—they feel understood. Let your child know their emotions, ideas, and opinions are worthy and it's safe to express them to you:

- "It makes sense you're angry. You didn't want us to split up."
- "It's okay to feel sad. I'm feeling sad right now too."
- "I know it's hard to say goodbye. I love you and will be happy to see you on Friday."
- "I understand. You're worried about what people will think if you tell them about our divorce."
- "You wish things were back to the way they were."
- "I know our breakup feels *so* unfair. It is frustrating and isn't something you chose."
- "Look at you! You're so excited to go to the beach with your dad."

Remember, validating feelings is not about what's right or wrong or about finding solutions.

Answer Their Questions

Children can ask a lot of questions in their effort to make sense of the world. Following a separation or divorce, and for years to come, your child may have many questions:

- "What did *I* do wrong?"
- "Will you get back together again?"
- "Can I keep my stuff?"
- "How will I tell my friends?"
- "Why did you separate?"
- "So, love isn't forever? Do any marriages last? What does this mean for me?"

Take the time to answer these questions to the best of your ability and in an age-appropriate and neutral manner.

In addition to these tools for emotional connection, there is one tool that deserves its own section: awareness of sensations.

Being Aware of Sensations

Perhaps you've heard the term *emotional backpack*. It refers to the places in our body where we hold our unprocessed and difficult feelings. We fill up our backpack with all the unprocessed emotions that got stuck in the body and carry it around with us wherever we go.

Suppose your child has to witness you and their other parent fighting or is subjected to hearing negative things about their other parent. Maybe they don't feel safe talking about their feelings or don't have a mindful and attuned adult around. So all that stuff lands in their emotional backpack. It's hard to feel free to hop and skip, run and play, when weighed down this way. Stashing your emotions this way doesn't make them disappear. They just go deeper and deeper into the body. A child whose emotional backpack is stuffed is likely to start feeling physical pain, such as stomachaches, headaches, sluggishness, numbness, nausea, or other symptoms. These may have no apparent medical cause, but they can indicate your child has feelings that need to be acknowledged and processed.

The good news here is that, while your child's body may be hurting, their body also provides a key for healing. This is because it is possible to gain access to feelings through their expression in the body. *Somatic Experiencing* is a method you can use to bring awareness to the sensations in your child's body, so their trauma and difficult experiences can be felt and completed (Levine and Kline 2008). This is especially useful for a child who is grieving a separation or divorce. Gaining expertise at this method is beyond the scope of this book, but the following exercise is a good beginning. Adapt it, as needed, to fit your child's age.

Drawing It Out

Doing these steps with your child can help them access and process their feelings. The only materials you need are paper and colored pencils, markers, or crayons, or you can use a tablet.

Ask your child to draw their emotions. Either you or your child can draw a human form. Then have them draw where in this body—their body—they feel various emotions. Allow them to choose which color represents which emotion. There are no wrong colors!

Once your child has colored their emotions in their body, they may feel more ready to talk about them. An older kid may be able to talk about where their emotions are in their body without drawing them. Saying something like the following can help you initiate this conversation: "Sometimes when we feel sad or angry or worried, we feel it in our body. It can feel like tightness or a yucky feeling in your belly or chest or head. When you get [mad or sad or worried], where might you feel it in your body?"

You can keep the conversation going by having your child say hello to their feeling. They can place their hand on the body where it hurts. Ask them, "Does your feeling want to tell you something about itself?" Or "Does it have a texture? What does it look like? Does it have a shape or color or temperature? Is it moving? How big is it?"

You can extend this exercise to focus on emotions related to your breakup, including your child's feelings about the future. Be sure to validate their emotions by saying, "I understand," "That makes sense," or "I believe you."

This exercise is about allowing whatever is there to be heard and witnessed, not about changing or fixing your child's feelings. That said, you may find that once a sensation is acknowledged, it starts to dissipate or move.

Keep in mind that the emotions your child uncovers may not appear to be related to your breakup. Your child may focus on frustrations at school or with a friend or a sibling. This is perfectly natural and fine. It may be easier for your child to use those situations to access their feelings right now. Any processing they can do will lighten the load in their emotional backpack and be of value down the line.

Kia and Zephyr's co-parents tried some of the tools we've been discussing, while holding space for and being mindful of their kids' emotions, to help Kia and Zephyr process their feelings. As you read these excerpts from their dialogues, see if you can recognize what these co-parents are trying to do and how it's working.

• *Mom's Dialogue with Kia*

After Kia's mother asks her to get ready for dinner, Kia says she wants to eat by the TV, not with her mother and brother. When Mom doesn't allow that, Kia runs to her room and throws herself on her bed.

Kia: I just want to be alone!

Mom: (Sits quietly on the edge of the bed) You're really mad right now. That's okay. I'm here with you.

Kia: (Fiddles with her coverlet, doesn't say anything)

Mom: (With a curious tone) I wonder what's making you mad?

Kia: (Snaps) I don't know.

Mom: (Pauses, then speaks softly) Are you mad about all the changes? You're allowed to be. I understand.

Kia: (Listening)

Mom: I know you loved that house. It was your home for so many years. So, of course you're mad. And maybe even sad.

Kia: Yeah. Because where will Dad go when he comes back?

Mom: Oh, I get it. You think if we kept the house, we might get back together?

Kia: (Nods, eyes cast down)

Mom: Oh honey, I know this is so hard.

Kia: (Wails) It's not fair! How do you know you won't get back?

Mom: (Puts her hand on Kia's back) Honey, your dad and I discussed that. We aren't getting back together. There's nothing you or your brother could do to change or fix that. The house won't make things go back to how they were. Your dad and I love you so much—to infinity and back. That love will never change, no matter what.

Kia: (Her body relaxes as she starts to cry)

Mom: I love you. I'm here with you.

Now let's look at what happened when Zephyr's dad encouraged him to express his feelings.

● Dad's Dialogue with Zephyr

Zephyr is doing the "Drawing It Out" exercise with his father. He chooses purple and makes a scribble in the abdomen area of his picture.

Dad: So that purple is what you're feeling in your stomach?

Zephyr: Uh-huh.

Dad: Can you put your hand where it aches?

Zephyr: (Puts hand on stomach) Here.

Dad: Hello, purple ache. Let's get to know it a little. Is that okay?

Zephyr: Yeah.

Dad: What does it look like?

Zephyr: Kind of swirly. Like a lot of sharp and spikey butterflies.

Dad: Butterflies?

Zephyr: Yeah, not the happy kind.

Dad: Do those butterflies have something to say?

Zephyr: (Thinks for a moment) I just wish you and Mom still lived in the same home.

Dad: I understand. Of course you didn't want things to change. It's painful, I know.

Zephyr: What if I hate my new school?

Dad: It makes sense you'd be scared about moving and going to a new school. It's okay to be scared. When I started my new job, I was *so* nervous. Your mom and I will be with you every step of the way. You're not alone, Zee.

Zephyr: I want to show this picture to Mom.

Dad: Great idea! (Pauses) How are the butterflies doing in your stomach right now?

Zephyr: They're not there as much. Can I play outside now?

In these two scenarios, the co-parents stayed calm and present with their kids and provided space for them to express the emotions underlying their behavioral and physiological symptoms. Mom helped Kia regulate her distress, which in turn allowed Kia to better receive support. Dad helped Zephyr talk about his feelings, guiding him to process them in his body. Connecting with your child through conversations like these doesn't have to take a long time, but it does take intentionality and practice.

Nurturing secure attachment with your child is one key way to help your child navigate the murky waters of a split household. But co-parents are not the only sources of support for a child. Nor are families static or isolated. As your family structure changes, it can continue to expand to include community and new partners. We will look at this expansion in the next chapter.

● ● Now What? ● ●

Question: "Whenever I try to talk with my daughter about our separation, she says she's fine. What should I do?"

Answer: Even if your child says she's fine, that doesn't necessarily mean she is. She may be in denial or may not want to bother you if she thinks her feelings will upset you. Either way, use your connection time to continue to pay attention to her underlining feelings and needs. Show that you respect her boundaries while also letting her know you'll be there when she's ready to share more. Once she feels safe enough to open up, she will.

Question: "Our kids don't know our breakup was because I had an affair. I don't want to cause more trauma by lying, so what do I say?"

Answer: You and your co-parent need to present a united front when it comes to answering difficult questions. Discuss what you both consider to be in the best interests of your kids, based on their age and how the information may affect your relationships with them. Sometimes information is for adults only, and that's okay. At other times, kids ask questions not because the answer will serve them but because they're confused and need reassurance. In that case, your answer should focus on how safe they will always be with you both.

Question: "My son talks freely to me about his emotions but doesn't talk at all to his other parent. Is this a problem?"

Answer: This is normal. Every child has their own relationship with each parent. This is true in two-home as well as one-home families. Remember, too, that a child needs only one secure relationship to thrive. Focus on cultivating a secure and connected relationship with your child, because that's all you can really control.

Chapter 9

Expanding Your Circle of Love

When I was hit with the reality that my marriage was ending, I felt utterly alone. How was I supposed to parent on my own? I had no idea where to begin. But then, even as anxious as I was, I did something I hadn't done before. I let people know I needed help. I geared up my courage and reached out to a mom in Ellie's kindergarten class and asked her to connect me with other moms who were separated.

She did, and I was amazed at how many of us there were. Immediately, I didn't feel so alone or ashamed. I made coffee dates after morning drop-offs, so I could gather information to help with the overwhelm I was feeling. "Do I get a mediator or a lawyer?" "What custody arrangements do you have?" I had so many questions, and these moms had many helpful answers. I gratefully accepted their offers to help, even though I wanted to act like I had it all together. And I got myself into therapy. I knew that if I couldn't sit in my vulnerability and ask for help, I couldn't be the mom I wanted to be or the co-parent I had to be. I couldn't protect my daughter if I couldn't support myself. To this day, I give credit to the community of people who helped me find my footing as a co-parent and with whom I continue to share this journey.

Peer-to-peer connection can help you heal more quickly and improve your overall well-being. Turning to a social network can give you a sense of belonging and a basis to develop and cultivate secure attachment when you aren't finding that in your two-home family system. And, perhaps most importantly, your child will thrive when they're encircled by supportive and nurturing communities.

In this chapter, we will look at the principle of *community*: co-parents build community and support systems, thereby fostering a sense of belonging. Expanding your circle of love with community is something you and your co-parent will each provide to your child. Having communities of support is a win for each parent as well as a win-win-win for your child. I like to view extended communities—which may or may not overlap—as solidifying the foundation of your co-parenting triangle, helping it remain strong for your child (see figure 2). First we'll discuss how to create circles of support for you and your child outside your two-home structure. Then we'll look at dating and how to bring in a new partner if the relationship gets serious.

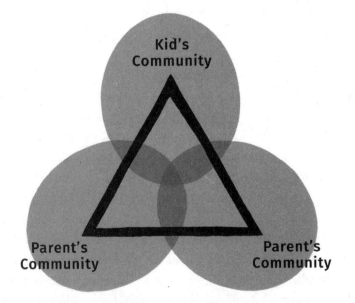

Figure 2: Community Circles

Developing Your Circle of Support

Community is formed when we build relationships based upon similar values, interests, and need-based resources and support. A colleague of mine uses the metaphor of a tree to describe the benefits of community: the tree's roots reach out beyond its trunk to gather more nutrients and water. In the same way, your "roots" can reach beyond your immediate family to a wider circle, so you can continue to grow and bear healthy fruit: your child, your creativity, your work, your life.

Your circle can include friends, extended family, neighbors, work colleagues, new partners, and cooperative-living arrangements. It can draw on social networks, such as schools, religious centers, gyms, and creative spaces. Therapists, support groups, and doctors can also be part of your community.

If you've recently separated, you may find your community and friendships shifting. This can involve additional losses, as some of your friends take sides or fade into the background. Some relationships may become more complicated. For example, while your ex-in-laws will hopefully continue to be a strong part of your child's community, they may no longer be that for you. At the same time, new people will enter your life, offering fresh insight, support, and care.

Connect with Others

Sit down and make a list of people you know (family and friends) who won't judge you and who will support you on your healing journey, including your efforts to build a healthy co-parenting relationship.

Divide these people into three groups (some may be in more than one group):

1. Your social crew: people you can meet up with regularly for an outing, such as looking at art, sharing a meal, setting up play-dates, seeing a movie, hiking, or bowling

2. Your short list: people you can call or text in any moment to lift you up, lend an ear, or give a fresh perspective

3. Your helpers: people you can call upon for at-home help (including last-minute requests), such as sitters, neighbors, extended family

Start connecting with people in each of these groups. Some you will see frequently and others less often, but all of them are essential parts of your community.

In addition to connecting with people who will support you, this is a good time to build community by opening yourself to new connections.

Meet other parents. Connect with other parents in your kid's school, at birthday parties, or on the playground. Invite these parents over or go out for coffee or a walk, either with or without your kids.

Join a group. Find groups in your area that align with your interests, such as a hiking group, church, the gym, or a creative class. You might find a support group for separated or single parents.

Volunteer. Find an organization that aligns with your values, and volunteer there. Some volunteer opportunities also welcome children.

Connect on social media. Many divorced- and single-parent groups are available online. While social media shouldn't replace human connection, it can be a great venue to normalize your experience and meet people in your area.

Just as you and your co-parent need social connection, your child also benefits from community. Let's look at how you can help your child develop their circles of support.

Expanding Your Child's Circle of Support

Given that divorce is so prevalent, and many people are turning to alternatives to traditional two-parent homes, many of your child's peers will also experience their family structures shifting. Awareness of this can normalize your child's experience: *It's not just me.*

Even so, creating intentional spaces for your child to talk can be helpful. Preteens and teens will likely have their peers and friend groups. For example, my daughter and her friend (also from a separated household) support each other. Referring to other kids' comments, the girls might say, "That's just because *they* don't understand. For us, it's normal." Their shared experience means they don't have to take on shame from other kids' discomfort.

For a younger child, you can arrange playdates. If you notice your child plays alone, find out what's going on. You can initiate ways for them to meet other kids their age with similar interests, such as through after-school clubs or activities. Supportive teachers and their friends' parents can also be part of your child's support network.

Bringing in a New Partner

You and your co-parent may seek belonging through new romantic relationships. Let's look at how you can create greater community and new partnerships in ways that are not disruptive to your two-home system and that will enhance not only your life but also that of your child.

• Sonya and Kalil: Take 1

Sonya and Kalil, who separated a year ago, were successfully co-parenting twelve-year-old Liba. They agreed neither would introduce a new partner to Liba before eight months of dating. But after Sonya had dated Eloise a short while, she brought home her "friend."

Liba mentioned to her dad that Eloise was hanging out a lot. "She tells me what to do like she owns the place," Eloise complained. "She's not my mom!"

Kalil was furious. He knew Eloise was Sonya's new partner, but he hadn't met her yet.

When he tried to discuss this with Sonya, she suggested he find a new partner of his own. "Don't be so uptight," she said. "Eloise is great. She already loves Liba."

"This is moving too fast," Kalil said. "Plus, we're her parents, not Eloise!"

Once you're a parent, you'll always be a parent to your child. That won't change if either you or your co-parent brings in a new partner. That partner enters a system that's already in existence: your triangle. Their entrance doesn't suddenly make the system a square or break up your triangle.

Of course, it can be complicated to navigate multiple relationships or see your co-parent with someone new. Or you may fully be on board with your partner's new partner but recoil at the idea of your child getting close to them. Alternatively, you may feel pressured by a new partner to choose them over maintaining a cooperative co-parenting relationship.

As discussed in earlier chapters, unplugging from your ex as your primary attachment figure will help you move on. However, the two of you may work through the phases of your grief cycles at different rates, and you may feel differently about introducing a new partner into the picture. Ultimately, if your new partner sticks around, they will become your primary attachment figure. That doesn't end your existing co-parenting team. Just as we maintain romantic partners and work colleagues in separate emotional and physical spheres, your partner and your co-parent can coexist without threatening each other or the well-being or secure attachment of your child.

Some parents date a new partner for a while and then move into cohabitation or remarriage. Others engage in serial dating or in polyamorous or open relationships. Yet others form other types of committed or uncommitted relationships. As a result, there is no single formula for successfully bringing a new partner into your two-home family. Here are some guidelines to consider. You can apply those that fit your life and relationship choices.

Keep Dating Separate

Dating is for you, not your kids. So keep your romantic life separate from your parenting life until something serious has developed. As we saw, Sonya created havoc by prematurely bringing her new date into her parenting time. You don't want your child to be confused by a parade of different people. Your child sees you as a role model. Adolescents, especially, will follow your lead as they start to explore love and sex.

As you move beyond casual dating, consider how a romantic partner fits into your triangle as part of your supportive community. Are you ready? Are they good for you *and* good for your child? Do they support your triangle?

Notice Green or Red Flags

If the new relationship is getting serious, you want to look for green flags. Use these criteria to see how your prospective partner measures up. Ask yourself if your new partner:

- Understands your relationship with your child is your top priority

- Is supportive of the quality time, routines, and structures in place for your child

- Respects that you have a co-parent with whom you are in regular contact and make all decisions regarding your child

- Shares your parenting values and parenting style

- Respects your child and their emotional and physical needs

- Offers a neutral or peacekeeping perspective; doesn't aggravate problems between you and your co-parent

- Supports your co-parenting triangle, does not undermine it

It's also important to watch for red flags. Ask yourself if your new partner:

- Makes you feel guilty if you spend alone time with your child and don't include them

- Isn't respectful of the space your child already has or needs in your home

- Expects you to change routines and schedules to meet their needs

- Competes with your child for your attention or affection

- Interferes with your child's relationship with you or your co-parent

- Stops you from interacting or collaborating with your co-parent

- Is too quick to assume a parental or disciplinarian role with your child

- Exhibits signs of abuse, aggression, or inappropriate behavior with your child

If you see any of these red flags, discuss them with your new partner. Decide if they present a reason to pump the brakes. However, if your partner is consistently waving green flags, they may be ready to meet your child.

Be mindful as you introduce your child to your new partner. Even if you know your new partner well and feel ready to bring them into your child's life, remember that your child is meeting them for the first time. Be sensitive to your child's concerns and talk with them about any fears or worries they may have. Depending on their age and where they are in their grief process, seeing you with a new love may be hard for them. They may be resistant and even hostile. They may see your new partner as the nail in the coffin that ends all hope of you and their other parent getting back together. They may feel a loss of control or fear being rejected or replaced. They may not be ready or able to recognize your sexuality. They may think that loving or even liking your partner will threaten their loyalty to their other parent, or they may feel guilty for liking your new partner because it will hurt their other parent.

Keep the Triangle Strong

If you and your co-parent work together to ensure your co-parenting triangle stays secure and consistent, adding an adult into your child's life can create greater community and support for all. Here are some guidelines to turn it into a positive for you and for your child.

MAKE CLEAR AGREEMENTS

Agree with your co-parent ahead of time to both protect your co-parenting triangle and operate from the same guidelines. Understand that you both have to abide by that agreement. For example, Kalil and Sonya had an agreement, but Sonya broke trust when she failed to follow it.

GO SLOW

There is no set amount of time before it's okay to introduce a new partner. Recommendations run from six months to a year, but that also depends on lots of factors, such as the age of the child and the amount of time following a breakup. Bottom line is don't rush it.

Surprises don't go over well when it comes to new partners. Talk to your child about the idea that romantic love can happen again, that relationships between adults can end but we can form new ones. And that a parent's love for their child never changes or gets replaced. Reassure your child they will never lose you or their other parent. They will always be your priority, and any new partner you choose will be good for you and good for them.

Introduce your new partner to your co-parent first, not for your co-parent's approval but for them to meet each other. This eliminates any need for your child to keep a secret and shows them that their parents are a united front. It builds trust with your co-parent, because they know who will be around their child. It also signals to your new partner that you and your co-parent work as a team.

MAINTAIN A BALANCE

Continue spending quality one-on-one time with your child, so they never feel second fiddle to your dating life. As you start to incorporate your new partner into activities with your child, don't start skimping on one-on-one time. If you maintain a balance in this way, your child will feel connected to you and not rejected or replaced.

Joining households can bring up space issues, especially if there are bonus (or step) siblings to consider. Make sure your child doesn't feel pushed aside in an effort to accommodate the needs of your partner and their child.

CLARIFY BONUS PARENT ROLES

At whatever point a new partner becomes an integral part of your household, clarify their role—both with your partner and with your child. This includes assuring them that your partner won't replace your co-parent but will support your child's relationships with both their parents. A bonus parent can champion your household guidelines and expectations but shouldn't be the enforcer. If bonus siblings are part of the picture, rules should be age appropriate and consistent for all children.

Allow your child to choose what they call their bonus parent. This helps your child feel some sense of control. Let them take their time and take the lead in forming a relationship with your partner.

Including your partner in your parenting life is important because they are now part of your co-parenting ecosystem. However, make sure you include them without creating division, competition, or reasons for more conflict.

TEACH COMMUNITY

It's never too early in life for your child to appreciate the value of community. Talk with your child about their expanding family and community and how supportive relationships can come in many forms—without ever replacing either parent.

Let's look at an alternative scenario in which Sonya orchestrated a better outcome for the relationship between her partner and her child and maintained trust with her co-parent.

• Sonya and Kalil: Take 2

This time, Sonya contacts Kalil before bringing Eloise home. However, because Sonya and Eloise have just started dating, Kalil objects. When Sonya suggests introducing her as "just a friend," Kalil insists that Liba will see through that. Sonya sees his reasoning and agrees to abide by their original agreement.

Four months later, Sonya texts Kalil: "Liba knows about Eloise and is ready to meet her. Can we set up a time for you to meet Eloise?"

Kalil agrees to the meetup and promises Sonya he will give Liba a heads-up that he has met Eloise. Shortly thereafter, Liba tells her dad she met Eloise. "Mom's girlfriend seems nice," she says. "I'm not psyched about having her around a lot, but I guess I'll get used to it."

Kalil says, "I know it's hard to get used to a new person. I'm glad you think she's nice. I'm sure she's already a Liba superfan, as we all are!"

"Okay, Dad," Liba says, "but she better not try to be my second mom. I don't need one."

"Don't worry, honey," her dad reassures. "You'll only have us two parents, always and forever. Eloise can become another adult who loves and cares for you."

Community comes in all shapes and sizes. The more you water the roots of your and your child's trees and foster supportive social networks, the stronger your trunks will become. Then you can move on with energy and fortitude. Your child will grow up to be a secure individual who feels protected by the multiple layers of love and support surrounding them.

● ● Now What? ● ●

Question: "I have my kids every weekend. If I can't bring a date home unless we're serious, how can I even date?"

Answer: Get creative and lean on your community. Have dates on weeknights or at lunch when your child is at school. Look at your list of helpers to see who can be there while you're on a date. Or ask one of your child's friend's parents about a sleepover at their house.

Question: "It kills me to see my child traveling to my ex-in-laws with their new bonus parent. How do I handle that?"

Answer: I know it can be hard to feel like you're being replaced in the extended family. After all, they were *your* family, and it can feel like an additional loss. But while you are no longer their daughter-in-law, you'll always be their grandchild's parent. If you want to maintain a relationship with them, send a note and let them know. You could arrange to meet at another time with your child or maintain the connection by sending them pictures and updates.

Question: "It's hard to see my child cozy up with their other parent's partner. What do I do?"

Answer: It is hard. I get it. You may not want your child to like them, or you may fear they will replace you, but your child can be close to your co-parent's partner without ever replacing you in their heart. If your child has any inkling of your feelings, they may feel guilty about liking your co-parent's new partner. Trying to damp down their budding relationship will put your child in an impossible position, and you'll lose their trust. So, stay neutral and allow your child to form healthy relationships with others. This will, in turn, increase the trust, safety, and security they have with you.

Chapter 10

Setting Up for a Bright Future

Creating a secure foundation for your two-home family can be a triple win for your child, you, and your co-parent. Over many years, mainstream culture has tended to emphasize the negative aspects of divorce, of being a single parent, and of raising kids in two homes. However, more and more, parents and experts are recognizing that a lot of good can spring forth from two-household family systems.

Five years into being a co-parent, I can sit back and see the ways my divorce provided my daughter with positive experiences she will take into her future. I think about the wins I have experienced and the wins I see my co-parent experiencing. I also hear adults describing alternative family arrangements that serve them well, and see more research beginning to explore well-being across diverse family structures (Jensen and Sanner 2021).

Here are some advantages—silver linings, as it were—for your child in a two-family household.

Greater attachment security. Living in two households where both parents commit to co-parenting, your child has more opportunities to develop secure attachment with both parents. One parent who was previously less involved in parenting may step up as a co-parent and become more engaged in your child's life. They may become more involved in parenting decisions and spend more quality time with your child, even if the time shared isn't equal. All this will help your child feel more loved, worthy, and secure.

Less conflict. While conflict can occur in any family structure, separation or divorce can reduce a child's exposure to conflict, thus decreasing their overall stress. This can lead to better developmental outcomes for your child, compared with outcomes for kids stuck in high-conflict two-parent homes. Many children who had to endure years of watching or listening to their parents fight feel relief when their parents decide to separate. When your child sees you happier apart than together, they will reap the benefits of your happiness.

More love. When you co-parent cooperatively and aren't engaged in constant conflict, your child is more likely to grow up believing *I am worthy, I am loved, I am safe*. This allows them to build confidence and inner resilience, which they can then take with them into the future. They also build a capacity for compassion. Having experienced grief and loss on a deep level, they can more easily connect and be empathetic with others who are going through difficult times.

Greater choice. A child who goes through a separation learns that love is not static and that one has choices. Seeing their parents end a relationship that was full of unhappiness and strife and move into a more harmonious co-parenting relationship shows your child they don't have to stay in a situation that is unsatisfying or even abusive. They gain the understanding that people change, and love can also change—that fairy-tale love is just that: a fairy tale. This prepares them for the reality that their own relationships may be hard and may not always work out, and that's okay. With the addition of new partners, they may learn that even if one love ends, new love can be found.

New paradigms. Your child can reframe the experience of "broken family" or "failed marriage" as a successful cooperative co-parenting family that models valuable relationship and conflict-resolution skills. Your child will thus feel freer as they grow into adulthood to redefine their own family, if and when it's helpful, as a structure that reaches beyond the one-home nuclear family paradigm.

More life experiences. When a child lives in two households, they have the opportunity to have a greater range of life experiences, which can cultivate learning, flexibility, responsibility, and an appreciation for multiple perspectives. Living in two homes may bring more loving people into your child's life, including more siblings, more extended family, and more friends. My daughter gained a sister from her dad's remarriage that she otherwise would not have had.

In addition to these benefits for your child, a cooperative co-parenting relationship has many benefits for you. It's less stressful than a never-ending conflict with your ex and allows you to focus on your life and on your relationship with your child. While not having your child with you every day can be hard, it can also open up time to prioritize your work, develop your career, enlarge your social network, find new love, and even take time to rest. You can model and teach your own values to your child as you heal, rediscover yourself, and grow into a better version of yourself.

By following the six principles of co-parenting described in this book, you and your co-parent can build a secure foundation for your co-parenting triangle. Cooperative co-parenting is a win for you and a win-win for your co-parenting team, which leads to a triple win that includes your child.

You start by acknowledging your own emotional landscape, by working on your own stuff and untangling your emotional cables from your ex. You make the choice to engage and listen, without taking on your co-parent's emotions, and to respond rather than react. In this way, you work on your own secure attachment, which prepares you to work with your co-parent in an environment of mutual respect and teamwork. You commit together to prioritizing your child; to providing them with the certainty they haven't lost either of you; to collaborating on decisions, using clear and respectful communication; and to building a consistent structure for your child. As you implement the six principles of engagement, you stay present and connected with your child, helping them to process their emotions and become a more secure and resilient person who can blossom within the expanding circle of their communities and walk with confidence into their bright future.

Acknowledgments

I'm a firm believer in the power of community. Getting this book out in the world would not have happened without the support, guidance, and collective wisdom of so many.

Thank you to my partner, James (JED) Donaldson. Your unwavering belief in me and support through this often difficult and sleepless writing journey kept me going strong every day.

Thank you to my daughter. I'm grateful for your openhearted joy, creativity, and intelligence. I love you to eternity and back, and then some.

Thank you to Jude Berman, my wonderful editor. You worked your magic—clarifying, structuring, and helping me succinctly turn my story, ideas, and passion into a practical book.

Thank you to Julia Gallucci, my dear friend, colleague, and fellow co-parenting mom. You generously provided feedback and consultation and shared your knowledge and experiences with me.

Thank you to Kara Hoppe, amazing friend and colleague, who told me "you have to write this book" and helped me make an idea into an actuality. Your generosity, advice, and empathy are a gift!

Thank you to my parents, Neil Heims and Iren Smolarski, who provided me with unconditional love and the grounded belief in myself that I could do whatever I put my mind to.

Thank you to my sister, Chloe Smolarski, for sharing your wise perspective and always being there.

Thank you to my beloved B and B crew—Kristi, Jason, Carrie, and Emilyn. Our friendship and playdates since the early days have been the best community and emotional support along my journey through parenthood, divorce, and writing this book.

Thank you to my co-parenting teammate, SW. You're a great dad. I value and appreciate how we have learned to cooperatively parent.

And much gratitude to Tina Payne Bryson, Heather Turgeon, Justina Blakeney, Eric Bergemann, Rebecca Louisell, Thanna Vickerman, Faith Hitchon, Kathleen Jensen, and Jimmy Lizama—who have provided valuable feedback, offered social media advice, and shared professional referrals as well as personal stories.

Thank you to Jennye Garibaldi and my team at New Harbinger, who believe in the vision and purpose of my book. I appreciate your patience and support.

Thank you to every one of my friends, colleagues, and community who have provided insight and meaningful words of encouragement and support!

References

Ainsworth, M. D. S., M. C. Blehar, E. Waters, and S. Wall. 1978. *Patterns of Attachment: A Psychological Study of the Strange Situation.* Hillsdale, NJ: Lawrence Erlbaum.

Arain, M., M. Haque, L. Johal, P. Mathur, W. Nel, A. Rais, R. Sandhu, and S. Sharma. 2013. "Maturation of the Adolescent Brain." *Neuropsychiatric Disease and Treatment* 9: 449–61.

Barton, A. W., G. H. Brody, T. Yu, S. M. Kogan, E. Chen, and K. B. Ehrlich. 2019. "The Profundity of the Everyday: Family Routines in Adolescence Predict Development in Young Adulthood." *Journal of Adolescent Health* 64(3): 340–46.

Baumrind, D. 1989. "Rearing Competent Children." In *Child Development Today and Tomorrow,* edited by W. Damon. San Francisco: Jossey-Bass.

Bowlby, J. 1969. *Attachment and Loss.* Vol. 1, *Attachment.* New York: Basic Books.

———. 1988. *A Secure Base: Parent-Child Attachment and Healthy Human Development.* New York: Basic Books.

Davies, P. T., L. Q. Parry, S. M. Bascoe, D. Cicchetti, and E. M. Cummings. 2020. "Interparental Conflict as a Curvilinear Risk Factor of Youth Emotional and Cortisol Reactivity." *Developmental Psychology* 56 (9): 1787–1802.

Doinita, N. E., and D. M. Nijloveanu. 2015. "Attachment and Parenting Styles." *Procedia-Social and Behavioral Sciences* 203: 199–204.

D'Onofrio, B., and R. Emery. 2019. "Parental Divorce or Separation and Children's Mental Health." *World Psychiatry* 18(1): 100–1.

Fisher, R., and W. Ury. 2011. *Getting to Yes: Negotiating Agreement Without Giving In.* New York: Penguin.

Jensen, T. M., and C. Sanner. 2021. "A Scoping Review of Research on Well-Being Across Diverse Family Structures: Rethinking Approaches for Understanding Contemporary Families." *Journal of Family Theory and Review* 13(4): 463–95.

Johnson, S. 2013. *Love Sense: The Revolutionary New Science of Romantic Relationships.* New York: Little, Brown.

Kramer, S. 2019. "U.S. Has World's Highest Rate of Children Living in Single-Parent Households." Pew Research Center, December 12. https://www.pewresearch.org/fact-tank/2019/12/12/u-s-children-more-likely-than-children-in-other-countries-to-live-with-just-one-parent.

Kübler-Ross, E., and D. Kessler. 2005. *On Grief and Grieving: Finding the Meaning of Grief Through the Five Stages of Loss.* New York: Scribner.

Kuppens, S., and E. Ceulemans. 2019. "Parenting Styles: A Closer Look at a Well-Known Concept." *Journal of Child and Family Studies* 28: 168–81.

Lamb, M. E. 2012. "Mothers, Fathers, Families, and Circumstances: Factors Affecting Children's Adjustment." *Applied Developmental Science* 16(2): 98–111.

Lamela, D., and B. Figueiredo. 2016. "Coparenting After Marital Dissolution and Children's Mental Health: A Systematic Review." *Jornal de Pediatria* 92(4): 331–42.

Levine, A., and R. Heller. 2010. *Attached: The New Science of Adult Attachment and How It Can Help You Find—and Keep—Love.* New York: TarcherPerigee.

Levine, P., and M. Kline. 2008. *Trauma-Proofing Your Kids: A Parents' Guide for Instilling Confidence, Joy and Resilience.* Berkeley, CA: North Atlantic Books.

Lisitsa, E. 2013. "The Four Horsemen: Criticism, Contempt, Defensiveness, and Stonewalling." *Gottman Relationship Blog*, April 23. https://www.gottman.com/blog/the-four-horsemen-recognizing-criticism-contempt-defensiveness-and-stonewalling.

Mermans, R. M. 2021. "The Five Cs of Co-Parenting During the Holidays." *Road to Resolution Co-Parenting Guidance* (blog). https://www.roadtoresolution.com/blog/coparenting/the-five-cs-of-co-parenting-during-the-holidays.

Mindell, J. A., and A. A. Williamson. 2018. "Benefits of a Bedtime Routine in Young Children: Sleep, Development, and Beyond." *Sleep Medicine Reviews* 40: 93–108.

Neufeld, G., and G. Maté. 2014. *Hold On to Your Kids: Why Parents Need to Matter More Than Peers.* Updated ed. New York: Ballantine.

Pew Research Center. 2015. "Parenting in America." December 17. https://www.pewresearch.org/social-trends/2015/12/17/1-the-american-family-today.

Prossin, A. R., A. E. Koch, P. L. Campbell, T. Barichello, S. S. Zalcman, and J.-K. Zubieta. 2016. "Acute Experimental Changes in Mood State Regulate Immune Function in Relation to Central Opioid Neurotransmission: A Model of Human CNS-Peripheral Inflammatory Interaction." *Molecular Psychiatry* 21: 243–51.

Sacks, V., and D. Murphey. 2018. "The Prevalence of Adverse Childhood Experiences, Nationally, by State, and by Race or Ethnicity." ChildTrends, February 12. https://www.childtrends.org/publications/prevalence-adverse-childhood-experiences-nationally-state-race-ethnicity.

Schore, A. N. 2001. "Effects of a Secure Attachment Relationship on Right Brain Development, Affect Regulation, and Infant Mental Health." *Infant Mental Health Journal* 22(1–2): 7–66.

Siegel, D J., and T. P. Bryson. 2012. *The Whole-Brain Child: 12 Revolutionary Strategies to Nurture Your Child's Developing Mind.* New York: Bantam.

———. 2020. *The Power of Showing Up: How Parental Presence Shapes Who Our Kids Become and How Their Brains Get Wired.* New York: Ballantine.

Tatkin, S. 2012. *Wired for Love: How Understanding Your Partner's Brain and Attachment Style Can Help You Defuse Conflict and Build a Secure Relationship.* Oakland, CA: New Harbinger.

Aurisha Smolarski, LMFT, is a licensed marriage and family therapist, certified co-parenting coach, and mediator with a clinical practice in Los Angeles, CA. She specializes in working with co-parents, couples, and individuals. As a mom and co-parent herself, she is very familiar with the challenges faced by parents raising kids in two households. For more than ten years, she has drawn on attachment theory and other modalities to help clients navigate their emotional whirlwinds and create a secure co-parenting family.

Foreword writer **Hunter Clarke-Fields, MSAE,** is creator of Mindful Parenting, host of the *Mindful Parenting* podcast, and author of *Raising Good Humans* and *Raising Good Humans Every Day*.

MORE BOOKS from
NEW HARBINGER PUBLICATIONS

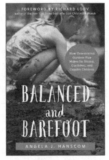

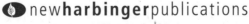